Pulaski, N.Y. and Vicinity

E. L. Welch

Alpha Editions

This edition published in 2019

ISBN : 9789353977214

Design and Setting By
Alpha Editions
email - alphaedis@gmail.com

PULASKI, N. Y., AND VICINITY

[ILLUSTRATED]

Dunwick, Photo.   PULASKI AND VICINITY.
Salmon River below Jefferson Street.   Jefferson Street (Long) Bridge.   Salmon River above Salina Street Bridge.
View from North Bank of the Salmon River, below the Village.
Famous Pleasure Island Picnic Grounds.   Salina Street Bridge.   Bluffs near Farrington's Grove.

ELIGIBLY located near the geographical center of Oswego County, one of its shire towns and at one time a rival of the metropolis of the county, Pulaski has advantages that many towns of its size in the northern part of the state might well envy. Largely an agricultural place, although possessed of manufacturing institutions, it has to draw from in the way of trade a section of farming country as good as there is in Oswego county and much better than in some sections of the adjoining counties. As the rule the farmers are prosperous and provident, realizing from their crops as good as the average. And the condition of the farming country is an index to the commercial standing of the chief town in that section.

Pulaski is the junction of railroad lines from widely separated sections of the state, making it easily accessible from all directions reached directly by any part of the R. W. & O. system of railroads, which is operated in close connection by the New York Central & Hudson River Railroad Company, lessees.

Here the road from Syracuse, 38 miles south, unites with that from Oswego, 25 miles west, the former closely connecting with the eastern and western trains on the main line of the Central and the latter with trains from the west via Lewiston on the Niagara, and Rochester suburban and other resorts and towns on the American shore of Lake Ontario. Only five miles east is Richland, the junction for the entire R. W. & O. system, Watertown being 35 miles north and Utica 57 miles in the opposite direction. By reason of its especially favorable location within its network of railroads Pulaski is in close touch with all parts of the state and can be reached as quickly as any other northern point in the state, not excepting Oswego.

The industries of the village are not varied but are on a sound, profitable basis and give employment to about three hundred people. The Tollner Box Works where are manufactured school boxes, cabinets and other articles of that sort which the public school children of the later times do not think they can dispense with; the Ontario Iron Works, where stationary engines are manufactured, and the Richards house dress factory where ladies' skirts and wrappers are made, are the chief establishments in the village.

Huested, Photo.   BOARD OF TRUSTEES.
N. G. Ehle, Clerk. Dr. J. L. More. S. R. Trumbull. Charles Hibbard.
Wm. Peach.   W. J. Peach, President.   F. G. Whitney, Corporation Counsel.

As a rule they enjoy a good trade the year around. Their stores are well supplied with the most desirable class of goods and they are the first to place on their counters the latest productions of the looms.

Society has its votaries in Pulaski who are known in wider circles of social life. The number of organizations formed for mutual advancement and evening recreation is unusually large. The young ladies of the village in their cooking clubs and their literary societies have found a profitable means of devoting their spare time.

Pulaski, however, has become widely known through the medium of one important if not large enterprise. F. H. Cross, who has devised an exclusive pattern of harness for those who are unfortunately crippled, has made such a success with his invention that he has customers who have come to him from the remote sections of the union. The genius that is shown by this man in his line has introduced Pulaski where it has never before been heard of.

Considerable dairying is carried on about this section and a great deal of cheese is manufactured here. There are also many fine strawberry beds where the best of the famous Oswego county berries are grown.

Pulaski has suffered in its time with some disastrous fires. The result is that the common wooden buildings so often seen in villages of its size have all given place in Pulaski to modern stone and frame structures, presenting to the visitor as he passes along the business street of the village, Jefferson street, a most pleasing as well as prosperous appearance.

It is the fact that the merchants are generally in good circumstances.

Their churches are alive to the best plan for self improvement and for elevating the tone of the community. They comprise the cultured classes and are well supported, employing talented clergymen to minister to their spiritual welfare.

The club life, while not extensive, as it never is in a town of this size, is of that intelligent order that inspires the members to maintain its best features. The Pulaski Citizens' Club, composed

Dunwick, Photo.   THE FIRE DEPARTMENT.
Top Row (from left to right)—Melzar Spink, Eugene Bonney, F. Brundage, F. E. Dillenbeck, James Manwaring, S. W. Holmes, Chief, E. H. Fuller, Charles Dodge, John Hohman, Frank Prouty, Eugene Miller. Second Row (from left to right)—D. C. Mahaffy, J. W. Parkhurst, E. M. Marvin, E. B. Walker, T. W. Shaul, Foreman, George Healy, G. W. Morton, Foreman, John Moran, F. J. Smith, Frank Scott. Bottom Row (from left to right)—L. Robarge, W. Vincent, Frank Bonney, W. Manwaring, Frank Lane W. T. Andrews.

of the business and professional men, occupies a suite of pleasant rooms in which the best games and other forms of relaxation are indulged. The reading tables are well supplied with the daily newspapers and all of the leading periodicals.

No better school in which the common and high school branches are taught can be found in any of the small villages of the state. The Pulaski Academy has long enjoyed a high reputation and many distinguished men and scholarly women have been graduated in its classes. —

One commercial advantage that Pulaski enjoys

village have found that natural gas was the cheapest and most convenient for both heating and illuminating purposes. The first well, on Mill street, struck the depth of 980 feet and during the ensuing night (so great was the supply and force) the drill, rope and 500 feet of casing were blown out. The well was plugged and work suspended but the company, the Pulaski Gas and Oil Co. (limited), of which L. J. Clark was president, held the franchise until the spring of 1894, when it was purchased by Charles Tollner, who immediately began drilling. The town was piped

Dunwiek, Photo.   GROUP OF STREETS OF THE VILLAGE.
Canal, Junction of Lewis Street.   Salina Street, looking North.
Upper Lake Street, looking East.   Church Street.
Mill Street, looking West.   North Street, looking South.

is the seemingly unlimited supply of natural gas which apparently underlies all of this section of country. Wells opened in various parts of the village to increase the supply as the consumption demanded have all yielded abundantly. It seems that nowhere hereabouts has the drill gone into the earth and failed to find gas in sufficient quantity to pay for drilling. Since 1889, at the time the original company of local capitalists was organized and began drilling, the people of the

and the result was so satisfactory that thereafter he had no difficulty in finding patrons and in a short time he had made it one of the permanent enterprises of the town. After his death it passed into other hands. From time to time new wells have been opened in the adjacent country, piping the gas to many of the country as well as village homes. It is furnished so cheaply to the consumer that many of the lights are kept burning day and night to save the trouble of extinguish-

Dunwick, Photo.   JEFFERSON STREET, WEST SIDE, 1902.

ing and lighting. It is regarded as certain that almost anywhere one chooses to sink a well within a wide radius of Pulaski, a profitable supply will be found. The capitalist has only to gain the consent of the farmer, and that is now generally procured at the cost only of lighting his buildings, to sink a paying well anywhere.

History of Pulaski. The founders of Pulaski were lineal descendants of some of the Pilgrims who came to the new world in the first voyage in the Mayflower and their names are Ephraim Brewster, who traced his ancestry to William Brewster; John and Simon Meacham, who were descended from Capt. Miles Standish; Gersham Hale, Philo Sage and David Kidder. Six sturdy young men were they, assembled on the pine covered slopes of the Salmon river, marking out each a site for a rude cabin. Leaving behind them in that staid Puritan (or Congregational) Vermont town of Pawlet their families, these men had made their way through the almost unbroken forests of Northern New York, planning to find a favorable location and prepare shelter for their families before asking them to share further hardships of pioneer life with them. They reached the present site of Pulaski, March 22, 1805.

The first white settler in Pulaski was Benjamin Winch, a surveyor. His log hut was the only building, the only evidence of any habitation which they found here. Proceeding to clear land they succeeded during the ensuing summer in building log huts, after which they returned to their Vermont homes. The following February, 1806, they returned with their families and thereafter made Pulaski their permanent home.

That year John Hoar and J. A. Mathewson arrived and by an arrangement with Winch took up their abode in the cabin he had originally constructed. Mathewson came from Rhode Island and was a native of Scituate in that state. He eventually erected a saw mill which was needed to enable the settlers to build such structures as they desired, the first mill in the village, and later a grist mill. During his later years he acquired considerable real estate in the town. His son, Jeremiah A. Mathewson, succeeded to his milling business and was for years one of the most prominent citizens of Pulaski, long recognized as authority in local history. The sketch of his life is published elsewhere in this work.

Immediately following the arrival of the Vermont party, in the summer of the same year (1806), five more families arrived. They were those of William Smith, Daniel Stone, Jonathan Rhodes, Rufus Fox and Erastus Kellogg.

Rufus Fox, who built his habitation near where the old Baptist church afterwards stood, subsequently took a place two miles up the river. Erastus Kellogg built the first frame structure in the village. It stood a few rods north of the present Froude block where he carried on blacksmithing for some time. William Smith put up a house near the present location of the railroad station and Daniel Stone and Johnathan Rhodes together lived in a log house. Three years later John Jones came from Oneida county, followed shortly after by Thomas and Rufus Bishop. At

Dunwick. Photo.   JEFFERSON STREET, EAST SIDE, 1902.

Dunwick, Photo.   LOWER LAKE STREET, LOOKING EAST.

mercial emporium. It was without question, a fearless rival of Oswego and was expected to leave that place far behind. While it was true that Oswego had the advantage of a good harbor, it was none the less true that Port Ontario, a very short two and a half miles from Pulaski was expected to afford a far superior shipping place as soon as the government had taken hold and expended the money which the few settlers of Pulaski were led to understand was to be the case.

On the other hand Pulaski then occupied a more favorable geographical position inasmuch as it was more easily and quickly reached from all sections of the county, being then considerably nearer the center and now almost quite at the center. There was a determined class of citizens who believed thoroughly in their own town and were always ready to make individual sacrifices to promote communal interests.

the beginning of the year 1810 there were less than a dozen families in the embryoic village of Pulaski. The present thriving village with its broad, well kept streets and beautiful homes and its large stores and public buildings, was then a hamlet of a few log dwellings, a blacksmith shop and a saw and grist mill—low one-story structures scattered among the pines which then grew in abundance along the banks of the Salmon river.

But in the spring of that same year the place assumed the dignity of a trading community. Captain John Meacham moved in from Sandy Creek with a load of merchandise and took temporary quarters for his store in the log house of Stone and Rhodes. A few days later he had constructed what was then considered a commodious building for his store at the corner of Jefferson and Bridge streets. The next spring Silas Harmon became his partner. They afterwards sold out to Milton Harmer; and Captain Meacham, the war of 1812 having been declared, retired from trade and raised a militia company which he led in defense of Sacket Harbor and Oswego.

Henry Patterson, who was a hatter, came to Pulaski with Captain Meacham. And about that time, too, there arrived Hudson Tracy and John S. Davis. The latter was the first sheriff of the county and was otherwise prominent both in town and county affairs.

The following year, 1817, the first court, at which a jury was drawn in the county, was held at Pulaski. This was in February. Pulaski was then the chief town of Oswego county and held a most favorable chance for becoming its com-

By prompt and vigorous action they secured the popular designation of their village as one of the county seats and in 1819 the court house was constructed. This important public utility has proven a bone of contention in later years, for as soon as Oswego had fairly begun to draw ahead of Pulaski in their race for commercial supremacy that city began a series of periodical agitations to have all the county buildings removed hence. The two shared the honors of being shire towns, county offices being maintained in both places, and courts alternating between the two. In the meantime a small but then ample building for the accommodation of the county clerk was

Dunwick, Photo.   PARK STREET, CORNER OF ERIE, LOOKING EAST.

erected next west of the court house, and the two oddly paired buildings, one towering fifty feet, more or less, above the other and the two just as different in appearance architecturally as can be imagined, for years stood in a conspicuous position overlooking the public square (the same occupied by the court house today), landmarks of interest to visitors.

sively owned by J. A. Mathewson, Arthur and Charles Mathewson, Porter & Ellis, Porter & G. W. Fuller, Johnson & Taylor, Johnson & June, Jeremiah A. Mathewson, George Woods and Dunn & Hohman.

G. W. Fuller had a potashery which was destroyed by fire in November, 1847; A. H. Stevens for many years conducted a hat factory, which at

PICTURESQUE AND HISTORIC.

From the "Democrat."

Old Light House at Port Ontario.   The Frary Dam.
The Salmon River Falls.   The Long Bridge, Jefferson Street.

The first physician was Dr. Isaac Whitmore, who came from Madison county and settled on the south side of the river in 1810.

In 1808 J. A. Mathewson erected a grist mill on the river on the site now occupied by the Tollner box factory and two years later erected another mill and in 1825 a third. A part of the latter was burned, March 20, 1890. This mill was succes-

one time was located in the building later occupied by George Washington on Broad street, and Hiram Lewis started a similar establishment in 1831.

Hudson Tracy and John S. Davis built the first carding and cloth-dressing mill which was subsequently occupied by Stearnes & West, in whose possession it burned in 1852.

From the "Democrat."
THE WATER WORKS.

A copy of the first paper, The Banner, dated Nov. 8, 1831, contains the following advertisers: John H. Wells, notice to delinquent debtors; D. Stillman, manufacturer of tinware; James Wood, proprietor of the County and Stage House, "on the north side of the river fronting the public square;" Benjamin H. Wright, land for sale; Ralph French, patent medicines; Hiram Lewis, "new hat store and manufactory;" Allen & Hale, merchants; Charles E. Barkley, painting and chair making; Luke Wood, tannery and shoe shop; M. W. Southworth, select school in Masonic Hall; Wells & Hall, general merchants; John O. Dickery, lottery agent; E. S. Salisbury, tailor.

The greatest period of Pulaski's industrial advancement in those early times, or rather the beginning of it, was in the thirties about the time of the establishment of the Eagle foundry and plow works. The use of machinery in agriculture was then confined to the most primative articles. About all that the farmers required was then manufactured in Pulaski and altogether by hand. The Eagle foundry, besides a general jobbing business, made all the plows that were used in this section. It was a large institution for those days. Under the management of Mr. Benjamin Snow the works were conducted on a large scale.

In 1831 Pulaski contained four stores and a half dozen mechanics. That year N. Randall started a paper mill. In 1847 the village was excited over a discussion for the construction of a plank road from Port Ontario through Pulaski and Pineville to join the Rome and Oswego road at Williamstown; also to extend the Salina and Central Square road to Watertown. That year S. Cook was running a distillery in the village. The Sal-

mon River Plank Road company was organized the same year.

The firm of Tallmadge, Wright & Co., owners of the Pulaski paper mill, was composed of D. P. Tallmadge, William E. Wright and William H. Gray. The partnership was dissolved Oct. 28, 1847, and Mr. Wright continued the manufacture of paper alone. Some years later Anson Gates Olmstead, of Pulaski, was a partner in the business for a short time. During the first few years of its history this establishment was a large plant turning out large quantities of paper.

About this time the local newspaper announces that H. N. Wright has discontinued giving credit for postage stamps, "except in emergencies."

In 1850 the O'Reilly line of telegraph was completed through Pulaski from Syracuse to Watertown. The population of the village was then 1,232.

Of the other early enterprises in Pulaski may be mentioned Lafayette Alfred's sash and blind factory started in 1848, Dr. L. S. Landon wool carding in 1851, Ingersoll & Osgood's carriage factory, Benjamin Dow's machine shop, the Empire machine shop conducted by David Bennett, jr., and Alfred Maltby, and the old Eagle oil mill leased by G. B. Griffin who was succeeded in April, 1854, by A. B. Collins and A. M. Duncan.

The book board mill owned by A. H. Stevens burned down, Nov. 10, 1854,

Pulaski village was incorporated April 26, 1832. In 1839 the limits were enlarged to its present size. On April 18, 1838, the charter was amended giving the village authorities more power relative to walks and streets and for other improvements, and to enforce such ordinances as they might enact to protect the health of the community. This was followed, May 25, 1858, by a re-incorporation. On March 24, 1871, the charter was amended giving power to grant licenses, and on March 29, 1883, another amendment was secured placing the cemetery under the control of three commissioners who were to hold office each three years. On April 10, 1834, the charter was again amended and on June 3, of the same year it was voted to incorporate under the laws of 1870.

From the "Democrat." THE OLD SALMON RIVER HOUSE.

Huested, Photo.   PULASKI LODGE, No. 415, F. & A. M.

1, Elvin G. Potter, Trustee; 2, George H. Fuller, Treasurer; 3, Louis J. Clark, Chaplain; 4, Benjamin Snow, Secretary; 5, David C. Mahaffy, Trustee; 6, Charles E. Low, S. D.; 7, Herman S. Killam, S. W.; 8, Thomas S. Meacham, W. M.; 9, Henry C. Twitchell, J. W.; 10, Minor J. Terry, J. D.; 11, Lewis J. Maey, Marshall; 12, Byron G. Seamans, Orator; 13, W. Fayette Austin, Trustee; 14, Labon D. Soule, J. M, C.; 15, Wilfred J. Lane, Tiler.

Pulaski Lodge, No. 415, F. & A. M.—Nearly a half century has elapsed since a number of Free Masons, residents of this and adjoining towns, desirous of founding a Masonic home, petitioned for a dispensation permitting the existence of Pulaski Lodge. The dispensation contained the names of Warren K. Combs, Frances L. Williams and Albert H. Weed who were master and wardens in the order named, and was dated August 11, 1856. The first communication was held August 23, 1856, at which Norman Root was elected treasurer and Augustus Day secretary. Don A. King, Frank S. Low and James A. Clark were among the first petitioners for mambership. The lodge charter was dated June 10, 1857, and contained the names of Warren K. Combs, W. M.; Don A. King, S. W.; and Peter M. Borland, J. W.; and was received August 19, 1857, when a communication was held to install officers. At this communication James A Clark was elected treasurer and Jesse W. Cross secretary. The installing officer was R. W. Luther H. Conklin. A large delegation of officers and members of the nearest lodges were present. The large hall in the third story of what is now called the "Froude Block" was the home of the lodge for a quarter of a century. On September 21, 1864, the members residing at Sandy Creek withdrew and instituted Sandy Creek Lodge No. 564, thus forming the

masonic relationship of mother and daughter. On September 19, 1883, the lodge removed to the Parkhurst Block where a most convenient hall had been arranged and for about ten years occupied it with pleasure and profit. During the occupancy of the Parkhurst Hall the matter of erecting a temple devoted exclusively to masonic purposes was discussed and in the year 1890 W's Oron V. Davis and Louis J. Clark and Brother Edward F. Kelley were appointed a committee to secure a plan and erect the present beautiful and most convenient Masonic Temple. The corner stone was laid on Wednesday afternoon June 15, 1892. W. Oron V. Davis was honored in representing the M. W. G. M., end qualified brethren inrepresenting the officers of the M. W. G. L. There were more than three hundred members of the order and a large number of citizens in attendance. The copper box placed beneath the cornerstone contains a miscellaneous assortment of historical records and appropriate articles. A fine address was delivered by Brother Edward F. Kelley. So entirely competent were the members of the building committee that the temple was ready for occupancy January 4, 1893. It was appropriately dedicated Thursday February 2, 1893. The R. W. H. W. Greenland D. D. G. M. of this Masonic district as representative of the M. W. G. M. arranged the order of exercises. Members of the

From the "Democrat."   THE MASONIC TEMPLE.

Huested, Photo.   PULASKI CHAPTER, No. 279, R. A. M.

1, Edward D. Fitch, M. 1st V.; 2, John Maguire, M. 2d V.; 3, Freelon J. Davis, P. S.; 4, Henry C. Twitchell, K.; 5, Louis J. Clark, E. H. P.; 6, Byron G. Seamans, S.; 7, Newton G. Eble, C. H.; 8, Ervin H. Andrews, M. 3d V.; 9, Richard W. Box, Treas.; 10, Oron V. Davis, Sec'y; 11, Marshall B. Lightall, R. A. C.

Grand High Priest, by virtue of a dispensation issued by James E. Morrison, Grand High Priest of the Grand Chapter of the state of New York, consent having been given by Mexico Chapter, No. 1.5, Darius Chapter, No. 144 at Camden and Adams Chapter, No. 205. The following were installed council officers: lewis J. Macy, high priest; Wilson F. Purdy, king; and Henry H. Potter, scribe. Twenty-one petitions for the degrees were presented that evening. About fifty Royal Arch Masons were present from Syracuse, Oswego, Mexico, Sandy Creek, Adams, Pulaski and other places. The ceremonies of the evening were concluded with a banquet at one of the hotels in the village. The dispensation expired December 27 of that year at which time twenty-eight convocations had been held and the membership was thirty-four. At the annual convocation of the Grand Chapter held in Albany, February 1886, the chapter was assigned the number 279 and granted a regular charter.

Pulaski Chapter, No. 279, was duly constituted, Monday evening, February 22, 1886. The following companions composed the council: Lewis J. Macy, high priest; Wilson F. Purdy, king; and Seneca D. Moore, scribe. Six petitions were

order, their families and invited guests filled the temple to repletion. Every detail had received proper attention and nothing was wanting to crown the exercises with success. The address by R. W. H. W. Greenland and the historical summary by Brother Edward F Kelley were scholarly, instructive and excellent productions. The exercises concluded with a banquet enjoyed by all. The lodge has a membership of 217, and has the reputation of being one of the brightest country lodges within our great state. The officers: W. M., Thomas S. Meacham; S. W., Herman S. Killam; J. W., Henry C. Twitchell; treasurer, George H. Fuller; secretary, Benjamin Snow; S. D., Charles E. Low; J. D., Minor J. Terry; S. M. C., G. E. Buck; J. M. C., Laban D. Soule; Chaplain, Louis J. Clark; Marshal, Lewis J. Macy; Tiler, Wilfred I. Lane; Trustees, Elvin G. Potter, David C. Mahaffy, W. Fayette Austin.

Pulaski Chapter, U. D., Royal Arch Masons, was instituted in Masonic Hall, southwest corner of Park and Jefferson streets, Wednesday evening, July 8, 1885, by Richard H. Huntington, Deputy

Huested, Photo.   PULASKI CHAPTER, No. 150, O. E. S.

1, Lucy J. Andrews, Esther; 2, Alice M. Brown, Electa; 3, Ida B. Hadley, Adah; 4, Wilfred I. Lane, Sentinel; 5, Zillah A. Rice, Ruth; 6, Eleanor M. Davis, Martha; 7, Mary A. Mahaffy, Organist; 8, Cora B. Macy, Conductress; 9, Nettie D. Holmes, Worthy Matron; 10, Simeon R. Trumbull, Worthy Patron; 11, Francis C. Davis, Associate Matron; 12, Ella L. Seamans, Associate Conductress; 13, Carrie B. Allen, Secretary; 14, Clarritta Parker, Warder; 15, Ella A. More, Marshal; 16, Carrie A. Twitchell, Treasurer.

Dunwick, Photo.   THE BAND OF MERCY.

1, Olive C. Richards, Treasurer; 2, Mary Jameson, 3, Maud Kelly, 4, Ruth E. Seamans, 5, Nina M. Seamans, President; 6, Yula M. Smith, Second Vice-President; 7, Bessie Shepard, 8, Florence C. Farrington, 9, Anna M. Clark, 10, Bessie Salisbury, 11, Beulah H. Dillenbeck, Organist; 12, Dorothy Felt; 13, Clara N. West, Secretary; 14, Edith Spolders, 15, Anna G. More, Vice-President; 16, Mae L. Pride, 17, Marie Hinman, 18, Winnie Daly.

The Sunshine Mission Band of the Woman's Home Missionary Society of the M. E. church was organized by Miss Flora E. Morris April 7, 1894, with the following officers: President, Jessie Warner; vice president, Mary Harvey; recording secretary, Allie Clark; corresponding secretary, Lena McKie; treasurer, Mary Ehle; directress, Lizzie Bnrt. During the eight years of its organization dues have been collected to the amount of $35.00 and supply work to the amount of $100.00. The present officers are: President, C. Flossie Macy; vice presidents, Clara West, Jessie Lane, and Mabel Brown; recording secretary, Anna Dodge; corresponding secretary, Florence Frary; treasurer, Beulah Dillenbeck; program committee Kate Richards and Lulu Erskine; directress, Mrs. W. S. Rogers.

presented for the degrees and six for affiliation. A large number of Royal Arch Masons were present from the surrounding towns and the usual banquet and toasts concluded an evening important in the Masonic history of Pulaski. The chapter prospered from its inception and at the end of its second year the membership was forty-seven. Since the completion of the Masonic Temple on Broad street the convocations of the chapter have been held in that building. Gradual additions have increased the membership to one hundred and twelve in good and regular standing. Those who have been elected and installed to preside in the chapter and received the order of high priesthood are: Lewis J. Macy, Louis J. Clark, Oron V. Davis, Edward F. Kelley, George H. Fuller, William H. Austin, Henry C. Twitchell, and Simeon R. Trumbull. The officers for 1902 are: Louis J. Clark, E. H. P.; Henry C. Twitchell, K.; Byron G. Seamans, S.; Richard W. Pox, treasurer; Oron V. Davis, secretary; Newton G. Ehle, C. H.; Freelon J. Davis, P. S.; Marshall B. Lighthall, R. A. C.; Ervin H. Andrews, M. 3d V.; John Maguire, M. 2d V.; Edward D. Fitch, M. 1st V.; Benjamin Snow, chaplain; Wilfred I. Lane, sentinel.

Prominent Missionary. — One of Pulaski's most prominent clergymen in the early history of the village was the Rev. Thomas Salmon, who was a scholar as well as a preacher, and who for nearly twenty years was a missionary in India and Ceylon. He was called to the Congregational church in Pulaski in May, 1846, and lived in the village, preaching the gospel, until he died, Dec.

Dunwick, Photo.   THE SUNSHINE MISSION BAND.

1, Clara West, First Vice President; 2, Olive Richards, 3, Anna Dodge, Recording Secretary; 4, Kate Richards, 5, Lulu Erskine, 6, Edith Scriber, 7, Kathleen Mahaffy, 8, Mae Pride, 9, Beulah Dillenbeck, Treasurer; 10, Margaret Brown, 11, Mrs. Alice Morris Rogers, Directress; 11, C. Flossie Macy, President; 13, Hazel Robbins; 14, Althea Orton, 15, Grace Utley.

Huested, Photo.   THE COOKING CLUB.

1, Edith W. Nye, 2, Laura B. Wilson, 3, Mary L. Dunwick, 4. Mame E. Warner, 5, Rena A. Naylor, 6, Florence E. Andrews, 7, Maud Potter Bonney, 8, Pearl Goodrich, 9, Jessie A. Warner, 10, Bessie L. Davis, 11, Dora E. Naylor, 12, Cora Robbins Sherwood, 13, Edith L. Wightman.

4, 1854. During his pastorate 89 united with the church. He was born at Tretford, Norfolk, England, Sept. 9, 1800, and went to India as a missionary when he was twenty-four years old. Coming to this country in 1842, he first preached at Trenton, N. J.. He was a proficient scholar in the Hindoostan tongue and assisted in translating the Bible in fourteen languages. His daughter, Mrs. Slater, is still living in Pulaski.

The Junior Kooking Klub - The idea that a Junior Kooking Klub was the one and only organization that could satisfy the hearts of young Pulaski girls became firmly rooted in the minds of Edith Naylor and Katherine Wright in December of 1901. Accordingly they invited six of their friends, Lillie McChesney, Eva Brown, Lulu Erskine, Lena Salisbury, Mabel Duane and Helen Woods to join them. These in turn voted to ask Irene Noyes, Anna Dodge, Mabel Hardie, Frances Mahaffy and Emily Clark to become members. This is our complete list of members—fourteen in all; but one, Mabel Duane, is living out of town at present. By vote a meeting was called in the High school building in the first part of January. At this meeting Miss Helen J. Woods was elected president and Miss Mabel A. Hardie, vice president. These being the only officers deemed necessary, the

meeting was opened to discussion and suggestion. Since that time a secretary and a treasurer have become indispensable in consequence of which fact Miss Katherine Wright was elected to the former office and Miss Edith Naylor to the latter. At this same business session it was decided that meetings should be held regularly, as far as possible, once in three weeks on Saturday; that they should be held at the homes of the different members in the aphabetical order of their names; that the hostess should decide what each member should contribute in order that she might make her own menu; that each dish must be prepared without exception by the girl assigned, alone; and that the object of the Klub should be to promote knowledge of the culinary art among its members.

We assembled for our first spread on Feb. 1, 1902, at Eva Brown's home on Lake street. The attendance here was complete excepting two who were unable to attend. The articles of cookery were all pronounced surprisingly successful and the conviviality of the occasion was also considered quite encouraging. To be sure, some of our members suffered from the quantity (*not* quality) of food eaten, but this proved to be nothing serious.

Since the first delightful assemblage, meetings have been held with Irene Noyes, Emily Clark,

Huested, Photo.   THE JUNIOR KOOKING KLUB.

1, Lena Belle Salisbury, 2, Anna Gertrude Dodge, 3, Lula Belle Erskine, 4, Irene Bernice Noyes, 5, Eva Genieve Brown, 6, Edith Grace Naylor, Treasurer; 7, Katharine Jane Wright, Secretary; 8, Helen Jeanette Woods, President; 9, Lillie Belle McChesney, 10, Emily Lucretia Clark,

Dunwick Photo.   PULASKI LODGE NO. 648, I. O. O. F.

1, Frank Lane, L. S. S.; 2, L. A. Knowlton, R. S. S.; 3, Frank Prouty, O. G.; 4, A. M. Frankenstein, I. G.; 5, L. D. Sage, Conductor; 6, Fred W. Jones, Rec. Sec'y; 7, A. B. Frary, R. S. V. G.; 8, George Cooper, V. G.; 9, S. E. Stewart, L. S. N. G.; 10 Wallace Hall, Chaplain; 11, J. W. Parkhurst, Warden; 12, Jacob Mickel, Treas.; 13, Albert A. Clifford, R. S. N. G.; 14, H. A. Wightman, N. G.; 15, S J. Clyde, L. S. N. G.; 16, E. B. Walker, Past Grand.

was granted Feb. 28, 1893, and the lodge was instituted June 9, 1893, by D. D. G. P., H. D. C. Phelps of Oswego. The charter members were G. F. Adams, C. B. Burch, J. H. Mickel, B. E. Parkhurst, J. W. Runyon, A. A. Clifford, W. G. Scott, F. M. Moore, M. J. Mitchell, Albert Wright and W. J. Sprague. The first officers were: C. P., G. F. Adams; H. P., M. J. Mitchell; S. W., F.M. Moore; scribe, C. B. Burch; treasurer, J. H. Mickel; J.W., B.E. Parkhurst; I. S., J. W. Runyon; O. S., H.J. Howlett; guide, R. E. Trumbull; first watch, W.J. Sprague; second watch, Albert Wright; third watch, F. L. Wright; fourth watch, A. A. Clifford.

The Past Chief Patriarchs in order of service are: G. F. Adams, F. M. Moore, B. E. Parkhurst, C. B. Burch, R.E. Trumbull, J. H. Mickel, H. J. Howlett, W. J. Sprague, J. W. Runyon, A. A. Clifford, G. H. Beeman, H. W. Robinson, P. C. Stewart, C. B. McLane.

The present officers are: C. P., H. W. Robinson; S. W., Frank Lane; H. P., E. L. Whitney; scribe, H. J. Howlett; treasurer, H. A. Wightman; J. W., S. W. Wyman; guide, A. W. Wright; I. S., G. L. Mattison; O. S., J. H. Mickel; first watch, J. W. Runyon; second watch, Frank Wright; third watch, F. V. Ballou; fourth watch, F. M. Moore. The encampment meets every

Anna Dodge, Lulu Erskine, Frances Mahaffy and Lillie McChesney, respectively. Visitors have at various times been privileged to attend and they invariably give evidence as to the unmistakable talent displayed by our members in all attempts at preparing delicacies.

Last spring it was voted to discontinue the meetings through the summer as many of the members were to be out of town. It having been decided that the Klub should camp out one week each summer and display the abilities of the members in preparing food for camp, a week the past summer was spent at Texas.

The Klub has certainly been instrumental in developing the taste for cookery among its members, and not only has it advanced their capabilities in this direction but it has also benefitted us socially. An outsider might easily become convinced of this fact were he permitted to enjoy one of our highly profitable meetings.

Salmon River Encampment, No. 31, I. O. O. F., was organized by a committee from Pulaski Lodge No. 648, Spring Brook Lodge No. 616, and Welcome Lodge, No. 783, appointed to enroll members. It's charter

Huested, Photo   SALMON RIVER ENCAMPMENT NO. 31, I. O. O. F.

1, Leonard A. Knowlton, 2, Harlan J. Howlett, 3, Frank E. Wright, 4, Jefferson W. Runyon, 5, Fred M. Moore, 6, Harmon A. Wightman, 7, Calvin B. Burch, District Deputy, Oswego County, 8, Sherman W. Wyman, 9, Ernest L. Whitney, 10, Albert W. Wright, 11, Herbert W. Robinson, Chief Patriarch, 12, John W. Parkhurst.

Huested, Photo. RISING SUN REBEKAH LODGE NO. 149

1, Mrs. Charlotte Frary. O. G.; 2, Mrs. George Haggerty, Treas.; 3, Mrs. Mina Clyde, R. S. N. G.; 4, Miss Kate Haggerty, Fin. Sec.; 5, Mrs. Mahala Mickel, I. G.; 6, Mrs. Nellie Harrington, R. S. V. G.; 7, Mrs. Cora Clifford, L. S. V. G ; 8, Addie M. Walker, V. G.; 9, Mrs. Lillian K. Decatur, N. G.; 10, Mrs. Lizzie Darling, Chap.; 11, Mrs. Jennie Beeman, V. G.; 12, Miss Edith Wightman, Sec'y (substitute); 13, Mrs. Marcia Knowlton, C.; 14, Mrs. Helen Hutchens, W.

first and third Friday of each month in Odd Fellows' Hall, Parkhurst block.

The subordinate lodges from which Salmon River Encampment draws its members are at present: Pulaski Lodge No. 648, Spring Brook Lodge No. 641, Iroquois Lodge No. 693, and Welcome Lodge No. 783. Although the encampment members are scattered through three towns, the attendance is good and the best of friendly relations exist among its members.

Pulaski, N. Y., Rising Sun Rebekah Degree Lodge, No.149, I. O. O. F., was instituted May 10, 1899, in Odd Fellows' Hall. The charter members were: Mr. and Mrs. B. E. Parkhurst, Mr. and Mrs. A. I. Decatur, Mr. and Mrs. S. J. Clyde, Mr. and Mrs. E. B. Walker, Mr. and Mrs. C. B. Burch. In 1900 Mrs. C. B. Burch held the office of District Vice-President. This lodge has a membership of 80, and has instituted and named Mexico lodge, Silver Crest, March 15, 1900, also lodges at Orwell, Richland and Lacona. The degree work of our lodge has been a success in every way. The past noble grands of our

lodge are: Mrs. C. B. Burch, Mrs. S. J. Clyde and Mrs. E. B. Walker. The present elective officers are: Lillian K. Decatur, N. G.; Jennie Beeman, V. G.; Maggie Jones, secretary; Minnie Hagerty, treasurer; Kate Hagerty financial secretary.

The appointed officers are: Lizzie Darling, C.; Helen Hutchens, W.; Marcia Knowlton, C.; Charlotte Frary, O. G.; Mahala Mickle, I. G.; Mina Clyde, R. S. of N. G.; Mina Stark, L. S. of N. G.; Ella Noyce, R. S. of V. G.; Cora Smith, L. S. of V. G.

Pulaski Lodge, No. 255, A. O. U. W., has always been a popular fraternal organization, and has numbered among its members many of the most influential citizens of the village. It was instituted on the 4th day of September, 1879, and its charter members were: L. R Muzzy, N. B. Smith, E. W. Peckham, J. W. Fenton, L. J. Macy, Rev. M. B. Comfort, R. W. Box, E. D. Forman, Dr. E. F. Kelley, A. W. Dunn, D. C. Mahaffy, W. F. Austin, B. D. Salisbury, Monroe Wright and E. M. Hammond, of whom eleven are now living Messrs. L. J. Macy, L. R. Muzzy, D. C Mahaffy, N. B. Smith, M. L. Hollis, E. F.

Huested, Photo. PULASKI LODGE NO. 255, A. O. U. W.

1, Leonard A. Knowlton, I. W.; 2, Thomas S. Meacham, Recorder; 3, John N. Daly, Receiver; 4, E. M. Marvin, O. W.; 5, David C. Mahaffy, P. M. W.; 6, Lucius C. Cole, Foreman; 7, Calvin H. Becker, M. W.; 8, Newton Philbrick, Overseer; 9, George H. Stark, Guide; 10, Nathan B. Smith, Trustee; 11, Frank B. Rickard, Trustee; 12, Lathum D. Potter, Financier.

Dunwick, Photo. J. B. BUTLER POST, No. 111, G. A. R. (First Group).

1, F. H. Cross, Serg. Maj.; 2, W. A. Austin, O. G.; 3, James Fellows, Guard; 4, J. A. Clark, Color Serg't; 5, Newton Philbrick, J. V. C.; 6, J. E Bentley, Chap.; 7, L. D. Potter, Q. M. S.; 8, A. N. Burr, Adjt.; 9, E. F. Morris; 10, S. Wolcott, S. V. C.; 11, H, B. Whitney, Com.; 12, H. W. Caldwell, M. D. Surgeon.

Cross, J. H. Bean, Z. A. Kiblin, H. B. Whitney, J. F. Box, Nelson Alsever, C. H. Halsey, F. H. Mahaffy and L. D. Potter. The post was named after J. Bradly Butler, who enlisted from this village in Company B., 110th N.Y.Vols., in 1862; was transferred to the Engineer Corps and was killed at Port Hudson, La., June 21, 1863. A.N. Beadle was elected its first commander and B. G. Reed was appointed adjutant. Their first campfire was held about the last of April, 1880, in the old stone block, corner of Jefferson and Lake streets, during which year the first Memorial Day address was delivered to the post by N. B. Smith. On March 18, 1881, the first death in the Post, that of B. G. Reed, who was accidentally killed at Clarksville, Mo., was reported. In the fire of Oct. 6, 1881, the Post lost all of its property except the charter, and after that held meetings awhile in the basement of the Baptist church, in the Methodist church and in the grand jury rooms at the court house. In September, 1883, the post moved into the rooms in the Froude block, formerly occupied by the Masons. On Dec. 26, 1887, occurred the death of Comrade A. S. Warner, late of the 147th N. Y. Vols. On April 16, 1889, J. B. Butler Relief Corps, No. 127, was organized by Mrs. Sarah C. Mink, Department President, W. R. C.

Kelley, John Daly and C. H. Becker have served as Master Workman, and to their earnest efforts much of the prosperity of the local lodge is due. Since its organization the lodge has lost six of its members by death: E. W. Peckham, J. W. Fenton, R. L. Parsons, Wells DeGraw, A. S. Lewis and D. W. Lewis, whose beneficiaries have received $11,000. The present membership is fifty-two, and the officers are: Past Master Workman, D. C. Mahaffy; Master Workman, C. H. Becker; Foreman, L. C. Cole; Overseer, Newton Philbrick; Recorder, T. S. Meacham; Financier, L. D. Potter; Receiver, John Daly; Guide, G.H. Stark; InsideWatchman, L. A. Knowlton; Outside Watchman, E. M. Marvin; Trustees, N. B. Smith, C. B. Hibbard, and F. B. Rickard; Medical Examiner, Dr. C. E. Low. The regular meetings of the lodge are held semi-monthly in G. A. R. Hall, and it is now known as one of the most pleasant and prosperous social organizations in the village.

J. B. Butler Post, No. 111, Dept. N. Y., G. A.R., was organized Aug. 27, 1879, with sixteen charter members, namely: A. N. Beadle, B. G. Reed, H. W. Caldwell, M. D., E. F. Morris, A. N. Burr, Judah Macy, J. M. Williams, F. H.

Huested, Photo. J. B. BUTLER POST, No. 111, G. A. R. (Second Group).

1, A. N. Burr, Adj't; 2, H. Douglass; 3, S. N. Hibbard, Q.; 4, R. E. Eggleston; 5, J. Macy; 6, S. Wolcott, Sr. V. C.; 7, I. D. Cross, Serg. Maj.; 8, F. M. Calkins; 9, L. D. Potter, Q. S.; 10, G. W. Seamans; 11, R. Young; 12, O. N. Sprague; 13, A. N. Beadle; 14, E. L. Burr; 15, H. B. Whitney, Com.; 16, W. E. Dunlap; 17, B. E. Parkhurst; 18, A.L. Sprague; 19, E. F. Morris; 20, L. C. Cole; 21, John Calkins; 22, W. H. Paddock, O. of D.; 23, T. R. Stewart; 24, F. H. Cross, Musician; 25, S. Doane; 26, L. M. Brown; 27, I. F. Hutchins; 28, A. H. Burr.

Old Photo.　JOHN BROCKMAN.

In January, 1893, the Post moved into the Austin block on Jefferson street. May 30, 1898, was a day long to be remembered by the comrades of the Post. With the Woman's Relief Corps and the Sons of Veterans and citizens generally, they proceeded to the cemetery where the ritualistic ceremony was read by the commander and chaplain. After strewing the graves with flowers the line was re-formed and marched to the opera house where the indoor exercises were conducted by Commander Potter. On May 11, 1901, the Post received a report of the death of Col. Henry H. Lyman, of Oswego, N. Y. He was president of the 147th Veteran Association, a member of Post O'Brien, No. 65, G. A. R., and a former resident of this village. On May 13, the Post had a special meeting to take action on the death of John Brockman. The total number of members mustered into the Post is 221; total deaths 33; transferred 51; now in good standing 79. The present officers of the Post are: Commander, H. B. Whitney; senior vice-commander, Sylvanus Wolcott; junior vice-commander, Newton Philbrick; adjutant, A. N. Burr; surgeon, H. W. Caldwell, M. D.; chaplain, John E. Bentley; quartermaster, S. N. Hibbard; officer of day, William H. Paddock; officer of guard, W. A. Austin; trustees, L. D. Potter, J. W. Wilder and H. C. Twitchell.

The commanders to date are as follows: A. N. Beadle, 1879-80, '82-'3; E. F. Morris, 1881; H. W. Caldwell, M. D., 1884-'88, '91; B. E. Parkhurst, 1889-90; J. H. Bean, 1892; G. W. Seamans, 1893; A. N. Burr, 1894-95; John M. Williams, 1896; S. N. Hibbard, 1897; L. D. Potter, 1898; William M. Hinman, 1899; H. C. Twitchell, 1900; Henry B. Whitney, 1901-'02.

John Brockman, who had the honor of being with Fremont in his early western exploring expeditions, was born in Hamburg, Germany, in 1820, and came to this country about 1842. Here he entered the United States service as a topographical engineer and was assigned to Col. John C. Fremont as his assistant in his western expeditions. Brockman accompanied Fremont in three exploring journeys. Receiving his discharge from the United States service at San Diego, Cal., in 1848, he went into the gold mines. In 1859 he came east overland, stopping at Milwaukee and then continuing on to New York where, in 1861, he enlisted in Co. B, 41st N. Y. V., and served during three years of the war, being wounded several times. Soon after the war he came to Pulaski and helped to start the tile factory which has been succeeded by the present Charles Tollner Sons' Co. Mr. Brockman, who was an honored member of J. B. Butler Post, G. A. R., was buried with the ceremonies of that body, his death occurring May 13, 1901.

Indian Fishing on the Salmon. So abundant were whitefish in the lake off the mouth of the Salmon river that during the season of 1851, enormous and unprecedented hauls were made. The Pulaski Democrat of that time reported that one seine took out 8,000 in a draw and another 2,000. The fish sold in the markets at three cents apiece. The salmon fishing in the river, especially a few miles up, was at that time on the decline. The oldest inhabitants remembered when great catches of salmon had frequently been made, and their fathers had told them of the periodical visits of the Indians, both from Onondaga and Oneida, and how they built their camp fires along the river; and on the morrow, after they had moved farther down stream, how the children of the neighboring white settlers came and with childish

Huested, Photo.　J. B. BUTLER, No. 127, W. R. C.

1, Carrie Burr, T. C. B.; 2 Alice Morris Rogers; 3, Mary A. Sage; 4, Mary Ehle; 5, Flora Tyler; 6, Ettie Andrews; 7, Ellen North; 8, Vytie Jones, S. C. B.; 9, Calista Burch Hibbard, Sec.; 10, Eleanor J. Stewart; 11, Nettie Parkhurst; 12, Addie W. Clark; 13, Carrie Twitchell; 14, Amaretta North, F. C. B.; 15, Martha Whitney; 16, Nettie Hillaker, Guard; 17, Celia D. Seamans; 18, Helen M. Box; 19, Anna L. Warner, Pres; 20, Delilah Hollis, S. V. P.; 21, Jennie Beeman, J. V. P.; 22, Emma Potter, Treas.; 23, Addie Doane; 24, Cora B. Macy, Organist; 25, Cora Smith, Cond.

Huested, Photo.
CALVIN B. BURCH, DEPUTY SHERIFF.

curiosity raked over the cinders. The big catches made at those places were attested to by the large quantity of cleanings scattered about, the Indians cleaning and drying their fish as fast as they were caught. Often their lodges were pitched in a favorable locality where they remained for weeks, many of their squaws being engaged in making baskets These parties always went back loaded up with their spoils of fishing. Farther up stream they carried down to the Oneida settlements large loads of baskets which they had spent the summer in making, the reeds being taken from the marshes which they had passed.

Calvin B. Burch, who for some years has been an active worker in the Republican party in Oswego county and who now holds the position of deputy sheriff, in charge of the court house and jail at Pulaski, was born in this village February 1, 1865. He attended the public schools and is a graduate of the academy in Sandy Creek, in the class of 1884. The following year, in 1885, he entered the jewelry store of C. B. Hibbard, which was then located in the quarters now occupied by the postoffice. During the ensuing four years his time was devoted to the interests of his employer, from whom he learned the jeweler's trade and for whom he also served as clerk. Then, in 1890, he became a partner in the business with Mr. Hibbard under the firm name of C. B. Hibbard & Co. In 1891 they moved across the street, thereafter

doing business together in the store Mr. Hibbard now occupies until 1896, when Mr. Burch sold his interest to his partner and retired from trade. In the meantime he had been appointed by Sheriff W. H. Enos as his deputy, and when Albert Warren was elected sheriff was reappointed by him, having served continuously in the office from the time of his first appointment; also holding the positions of constable and truant officer. Mr. Burch was elected water commissioner of the village of Pulaski in 1895, a position he held for three years, at the same time serving as treasurer of the board. He has figured prominently in local party matters, having attended county conventions as a delegate and in other ways aided to formulate and carry out the plans of county and town political campaigns, and is now an active factor in the Republican party counsels of this district. On July 27, 1892, he married Miss Gertrude Dunn, who was at the time a teacher in the Pulaski academy and who has made him a pleasant home. Mr. Burch is now a partner of W. H. Enos in the furniture business which the two gentlemen purchased of R. W. Box, and on April 1, 1902, moved to their building on Jefferson street, which they purchased three years previous and which affords them conveniences for a large store. His business engagements also include writing life insurance for the New York Mutual and the Phœnix companies. He is a prominent member of the Pulaski Lodge, I. O. O. F., and the local camp, Sons of Veterans, in both of which organizations he has occupied all of the official positions, and is a member of the Order of Elks, Oswego lodge. In Odd Fellowship he ranks foremost in this locality, holding as he does in the Encampment the post of district deputy. Mr. Burch's experience as a criminal officer has been very successful.

The County Seat Question has from time to time agitated the people of Oswego county who have differed in opinions respecting its location. Under the authority of the law erecting the county, enacted March 1, 1816, provision was made for two county seats, each representing one of

THE COURT HOUSE AND JAIL 1902.

the two "jury districts" into which the county was then divided. The naming of what was to be the two half-shire villages of the county was left to three commissioners named in the act, viz: Pearley Keyes and Ethel Bronson of the county of Jefferson, and Stephen Bates of the county of Ontario, appointed, as the law read, "for the purpose of examining and impartially determining the proper sites, in the respective (jury) districts in the county of Oswego, for court houses to be erected; and when the said commissioners, or any two of them, having so determined, shall put their determination in writing, with their signatures and seals affixed thereto, and cause the same to be filed in the clerk's office of the county of Oswego, such determination shall be final and conclusive."

It is fair to presume that there was some contest between some of the communities for the honor of securing one of the appointments, though at that time there were very few villages in the county and it is hardly probable that the commissioners named in the act had any difficulty in

constructed in 1887. It is a large, imposing edifice fronting on the public square. Until 1853 the records of the county were kept at intervals in places which seemed the most secure in Oswego and Pulaski. By common consent they were transferred from one place to the other with the election of a clerk, once in three years. By an act of April 11, 1851, the common council of Oswego was authorized to expend not less than $2,000, raised by a special levy of a municipal tax, for the erection of a fire proof county clerk's office in that city, which building was shortly afterward constructed, and there the records have since been kept. On April 6, 1852, the citizens of the town of Richland were also authorized to build a fireproof clerk's office on a lot given for the purpose by Benjamin Wright in Pulaski, provided that it be finished by September 1, 1853, and the town was authorized to raise $1,500 by tax. The supervisors let the contract for the erection of a one-story stone building to C. H. Cross and it was

Dunwick, Photo.   A NATURAL GAS WELL AND DERRICK.

making the selections they did—Oswego and Pulaski.

The construction of a court house in each of those villages was begun in the summer of 1818. That at Oswego was a wooden structure designed solely as a court house, although its basement was subsequently fitted up for a jail. The court house at Pulaski was a more pretentious structure, being designed to accommodate a commodious jail. The building committee of the latter consisted of Simon Meacham, John S. Davis and Ebenezer Young, the builder being James Weed.

In 1853 the old stone jail on East Second street, Oswego, was constructed, which answered every purpose until the completion of the new jail, in 1888.

In 1858 the board of supervisors appropriated $30,000 for the erection of a new court house in Oswego and $5,000 for enlarging and repairing the court house in Pulaski. The former was completed in September, 1860, and its cost was $610 less than the appropriation, being $29,390. The improvements on the court house at Pulaski were made in 1859. On the rear a brick annex was

completed in that summer at the cost of $1,295, on a site next west of the court house.

In November of the same year an effort was made to have the county seat located permanently at Oswego. This led to a hot discussion between those who favored and those who opposed the proposition. It became so acrimonious that the supervisors attempted to compromise by adopting a resolution, November 22, for the location of the county clerk's office at Mexico, it being supposed by those who favored Oswego that the people of that town might in that way be won over to the plan of making Oswego the place for the meetings of all of the courts.

The village paper at Pulaski opposed the plan so vigorously that a popular movement was started to have the county divided so that Pulaski should be the county seat of the new county. It went so far as to state that six or seven towns of the county "were ripe for revolution," and suggested that the geography of the county favored the division, erecting into the new county twelve towns with Ellisburg and Lorraine, Jefferson county, added. In the winter of 1853 petitions for the division of the county were presented to the legislature. In December, 1852, Judge Pratt granted an injunction restraining the county clerk from moving the records from his office in the city of Oswego. By subsequent action on the part of the supervisors and by an act of the legislature the permanent location of the county clerk was fixed at Oswego.

James A. Clark's personal history is inseparably connected with that of the town of Richland and the village of Pulaski, and the eminent services he performed for the town of his adoption, extending through the period of over forty years which was during the time of Pulaski's greatest growth and commercial importance, are marked by monuments more enduring than stone. The public school and the Congregational church held fast to his affections to the very last. No appeal to his loyalty to either went unheeded. Thirty years of service, 1855-'85, as a member of the school board testify to the public recognition of his sedulous and unwavering devotion to the interests of that important public institution. Its best interests demanded such men as he in control of its affairs, and his acknowledged financial ability and sterling integrity displayed in behalf of the public kept him for several terms in the position of treasurer of the board. He was one of the fathers of Pulaski's public school, and the high reputation it attained certifies to the value of his services. During eighteen years he was trustee and treasurer of the Congregational church and it was largely owing to his active and zealous efforts that the present hand-

From Old Photo.
JAMES A. CLARK.

some structure, in which that congregation worships, was built. The Pulaski National Bank, an institution which ranks high and is financially sound, as shown by its annual reports, is the creation of his genius and guidance. He foresaw the value of the enterprise to the community and the consequent liberal support it was bound to receive, conclusions fully justified by results.

During the last few years of his life he made strenuous though fruitless efforts to secure for Port Ontario, and Pulaski which would have been benefitted thereby, the re-opening of that harbor. He was satisfied that it could be made as important a port as there was on the lake, although it would have cost many thousands of dollars for improvements.

Mr. Clark was one of four brothers who, eventually, came to Pulaski from Unadilla, Otsego Co., N. Y. He was born in that village, Aug. 17,1821, and removed to Mexico, Oswego Co., in 1844. In the autumn of the latter year he came to Pulaski

seeking employment and found it in a clerkship in Frey Lane's general store. A year later he formed a co-partnership with C. R. Jones and the two carried on a general business for two years, when, in 1847, Charles A., Mr. Clark's brother, was admitted as a partner. Thereafter, during the remainder of their lives, these two brothers continued as close business associates. In 1862 they organized J. A. Clark & Co.'s Bank, an institution which they conducted as a state bank until finally it was re-organized as the present national bank. A brief illness found Mr. Clark still in the harness, his time engrossed with the manifold duties of the bank, and his mind occupied with other projects. After ten days of suffering he died, mourned by the community as well as his own family. His death occurred June 13, 1887.

Mr. Clark never cared much for political honors, although, like all successful men, when tempted into a political venture he fought with all his resources and he in no sense affected to despise popular approval. In 1883 he demonstrated his popularity by engaging in a contest for state senator with F. R. Lansing of Watertown, a foeman worthy of his steel. Mr. Clark was a democrat, and in a district adversely political with an opponent backed by a following such as a city like Watertown could afford, it was not expected that he could win. His own county, always strongly republican, had a natural majority of over 2,000. In spite of all this he carried Oswego by 2,400, and his standing in his party was justly recognized the following year by his being made presidential elector on the Cleveland ticket. Mr. Clark was one of the oldest of the fraternity of Free Masonry in this part of the state. He was, during the war of the rebellion, a strong war democrat, an upholder of the union who did all that he could to assist financially in furnishing men. On one occasion he pledged his personal estate as a surety for the payment of volunteers. When the town was bonded for the railroad he was made railroad commissioner, which position he held until his death. He left three children, Mr. Louis J. Clark of Pulaski, Mrs. Charles A Peck of Mexico, N. Y., and Mr. E. L. Clark, deceased.

Syracuse Northern Railroad.—Work on the construction of the Syracuse Northern railroad was begun May 18, 1870. It was opened as far as Pulaski by a special excursion to Frenchman's island, August 8, 1871. On August 26 following, the crossing of the river in the village by a train was celebrated by the citizens of Pulaski. Business was suspended. Mr. George Fuller was the first station agent and Addison S. Low was the

Huested, Photo.   PULASKI NATIONAL BANK.

Louis J. Clark, son of James A. Clark; his wife, Mrs. Ella M. Clark, and their three children. Mrs. Clark, the president, is one of the few ladies in this country who hold the presidency of a national bank.

In 1862 the Messrs. Clark organized the firm of James A. Clark & Co., bankers, conducting that institution as a state bank until three years later, when they turned it into a national bank. It occupies pleasant and prettily finished quarters in the main part of the building erected for the purpose, with an interior arrangement designed to accommodate its business to the best advantage. The president has for her private office a handsomely fitted up room, and lady patrons are provided with an apartment exclusively for transacting their business with the bank. The building, 60x60 feet, erected in 1883 of brick with Vermont marble trimmings, has two ground floor business places, one of them occupied by the post office, and is two stories high, the second floor being fitted up with handsome offices. The cost of the structure, including the best pattern of a vault, was $13,000.

Upon the organization of the bank Charles A. Clark was its president. He retired from active business life September 3, 1884, and James A.

first telegraph operator. The depot stood near the academy. The first through train for Syracuse left Pulaski November 9, 1871, at 11 11 a. m. and returning left that city at 3:28 p. m.

The Pulaski National Bank, one of the few banking institutions—if there be any others at all - owned entirely by the members of one family, was established by the brothers, James A. and Charles A. Clark, in July, 1865. They had been dry goods merchants for some years, having come to Pulaski from Unadilla, N. Y., and started in where Austin's meat market now is, in company with C. R. Jones. Then they went into business across the street next north of O. V. Davis' store, where they carried on trade as Clark Bros. Two years later they built the block where the Pulaski house now stands, which burned down in the fire of 1881. In 1865 they sold out their mercantile business to two other brothers.

From its founders the stock of the bank passed down to their children and grandchildren, until now it is owned by Mr.

Dunwick, Photo.   LOUIS J. CLARK'S RESIDENCE.

Dunwick, Photo.   CHARLES TOLLNER.

Charles Tollner, whose name stands foremost among the business men of Pulaski and its most enterprising citizens that have passed out of this life, rounding records of personal achievements which form a conspicuous part of the history of the town, was born in New York city in 1849. When he was fifteen years old, October 12, 1864, his parents moved to Pulaski where his father, Charles Tollner, for about a quarter of a century engaged largely in manufacturing, finally establishing the box factory which today bears the name of Tollner. Charles Tollner, the subject of this sketch, who was the eldest son, returned to New York when he was a young man, where he at first engaged in the hardware business at the corner of Broadway and Twenty-sixth street. Afterwards, in company with his brother Hugo, he went into the business of manufacturing frames for advertising cards and pictures. The two brothers, who were the pioneers in that line, made contracts, principally on heavy orders with the large concerns that catered to the popular fancy for gift pictures, chromos, fancy cards, etc., by widely distributing them for advertising purposes. The result was that Tollner Brothers built up a large business in that special line. In 1881 they dissolved partnership and Mr. Charles Tollner alone continued the enterprise which he largely increased by vigorous methods and natural business capability. In 1896 he moved to Pulaski to take the management of the Tollner Box factory, and in May of that year he erected the large and

Clark, the cashier, became president, Helen A., his wife, taking the vacancy in the board of directors occasioned by the retirement of her brother-in-law. Mr. L. J. Clark was then elected cashier and Edward L. Clark assistant cashier. Mrs. Helen A. Clark was elected president June 23, 1887.

The several officers and directors (who always included all of the stockholders), elected at various times from the beginning are as follows:—

The first board of directors (1865-7) were: Charles A. Clark, president; James A. Clark, cashier; Sherman Clark, Henry B. Clark and Samuel D. Bentley. In January, 1867, Sherman Clark, jr., was elected director in the place of Mr. Bentley, and in January, 1875, Mr. L. J. Clark took the vacancy caused by the death of his grandfather, Mr. Sherman Clark.

The next change was in January, 1884, when Mr. Edward L. Clark was elected director in the place of H. B. Clark retiring.

(Concluded on page 29.)

Huested, Photo.   THE TOLLNER RESIDENCE.

handsome residence on Jefferson street, which is still the home of his family. In July, 1897, his father died, and he and his brother Eugene bought the interests in the box factory which were owned by his brother Hugo and his mother and sister, who now reside in Syracuse. By this purchase Mr. Charles Tollner became the owner of two-thirds of the business, and to the time of his death was the head and controlling power of that large enterprise. He was also the treasurer and manager of the Pulaski Gas and Oil company's business which was established by his father. Mr. Tollner possessed a spirit of enterprise which prompted him in many ways to broaden any undertaking with which he was connected. He evinced a keen interest in the welfare of the village where he had made his home, and

ganizations was not large. He was a member of the Pulaski Citizens Club, the Oswego Lodge No. 271, Benevolent and Protective Order of Elks, and the Royal Arcanum of Brooklyn, where for several years was his home. His death occurred on January 10, 1902, after a comparatively brief illness which had confined him to his house less than two weeks. He is survived by his wife, who was Sarah M. Clark, of New York, to whom he was married in 1882, by their only child, Carl E. Tollner, a young man now attending school, and two daughters by his first wife, Mrs. Edith Sands of Brooklyn and Mrs. Grace Spolders of Pulaski. The funeral, held at his home, was largely attended by friends from out of town and the people of the village, the business houses in town generally being closed during the services.

Huested, Photo.   ORIGINAL BARGAIN HOUSE, J. L. HUTCHENS, Proprietors.
General View of the Block.   J. L. Hutchens.
Notions, Hosiery and Furnishing Department.   Dress Goods Department.

had planned personal investments which he hoped in the natural course of events would do much toward building up Pulaski and which were cut short only by his death. The fine building on Jefferson street occupied by J. L. Hutchens and the large structure at the corner of Broad and Park streets, in which the Pulaski Democrat is located, are monuments to his enterprise that mutely testify to the confidence in the future of Pulaski which he possessed. It was characteristic of him that the erection of structures on vacant property, whether for dwellings, stores or factories, by others as well as himself, gave him a peculiar satisfaction inspired by the sentiment he frequently expressed, i. e., that new buildings induced outsiders to move in and in the end promoted the welfare of the community, as well as proved a good investment to the owner. Mr. Tollner was open hearted, companionable and agreeable in his business dealings. Although socially inclined, his connection with social or-

Rev. J. Foster Wilcox officiated, and the members of the Business Men's association and several societies, as well as the factory employes, turned out in a body to do honor to the memory they all loved.

J. L. Hutchens' three large stores, occupying the whole of the ground floor and basement of the Tollner building (the largest business block in the town), have a high reputation as a leading place in trade and are widely known as the Original Bargain House. This large house was established by M. D. Cornwell a number of years ago. In February, 1886, Mr. Hutchens took a half interest and the firm of Cornwell & Hutchens extended their business until it was regarded as among the leading institutions of the town. In the fire of 1886 this firm was burned out and their place of business was afterward located in the Betts block. In October, 1901, when the new Tollner block was

From old Photo.
H. W. CALDWELL, M. D.

completed, they moved into their present quarters. On March 1, 1902, Mr. Cornwell retired from the partnership, Mr. Hutchens since then carrying on the business as its sole proprietor.

As has been stated, there are three distinct stores, though connected as one, having one large entrance. There is a French plate glass front of show windows 60 feet long, and each store has a depth of 60 feet. Besides the ground floor space Mr. Hutchens has the same amount of room in the basement, giving him an unusual amount of space, all of which he keeps fully occupied with his several lines of goods. These are arranged on the plan of the large, modern department store, which in effect it is, the stock comprising everything in the way of dry goods, etc. In the north store are the boots and shoes and cloaks, the middle store the notions, furnishing goods and carpets, and in the south store, dress goods. Following up modern ideas and the advanced position of trade, Mr. Hutchens has kept the people of Pulaski and vicinity in touch with everything new in his lines.

Mr. Hutchens was born in Union Square, Oswego county, N. Y., June 18, 1854. Horace Hutchens, his father, died in 1869, and his mother died in 1865. Bereft of his parents at an early age, he still kept at his studies, going through the district schools and in the spring of 1870 accompanying his brother to Baltimore, where he also took an educational course. In 1873 he re-

turned to Pulaski, where he resided in his early years and entered a clerkship in a dry goods store in this village. Two years later he went on the road as traveling salesman for the implement house of Whitman, Sons & Co., of Baltimore, Md., with whom he was connected six or seven years. In 1885 he married Kate D. King, and the following year began business in Pulaski, as has been stated.

Dr. Henry Williams Caldwell was born June 25, 1841, at West Monroe, Oswego county, N. Y., being the third son of a family of ten children of James G. and Eliza (Williams) Caldwell; grandson of Charles Caldwell, also of Dr. Henry Williams, surgeon of the Third Regiment, Vermont Volunteers, during the war of 1812. Henry W. Caldwell commenced the study of medicine in 1858 at West Monroe, with his cousin, Dr. H. W. Leonard, who passed away at Camden, N. Y., in January, 1901. In the fall of 1860, he went to Michigan and in August, 1861, raised part of a company and enlisted in Co. A, Eighth Regiment, Michigan Infantry Volunteers, as corporal. Dr. Caldwell was one of four brothers who enlisted in defense of the union. The others lost their lives in the service. While in action at the battle of Wilmington Island, Ga., April 16, 1862, he was seriously wounded, a minie ball passing through his right lung, and he was left for dead on the field. He finally succeeded in reaching the union lines and was sent to the general hospital in Hilton Head, S. C., remaining there about three months. Then he, with many convalescent comrades, was sent to Newport News, Va., but after remaining there a few days was ordered to Aqua Creek. On the voyage the vessel collided with another steamer, which soon sank, and he and about 75 others of some 300 persons aboard were saved. He soon reported to his regiment for duty; was made hospital steward and served as such through Pope's campaign in Virginia, and McClellan's in Maryland, many times doing assistant surgeon's duty, until the winter of 1863, when, being in feeble health, he was honorably discharged and returned to his home in West

Huested, Photo. DR. H. W. CALDWELL'S RESIDENCE.

Huested, Photo.
G. W. BETTS, M. D.

Monroe, where he resumed the study of medicine with his cousin. He took his first course of lectures in the winter and spring of 1864 at the Medical Department of the University of Vermont at Burlington; in the autumn of 1865 matriculated in the Medical Department of the University at Buffalo and was graduated therefrom, Feb. 21, 1866. On March 1, following, he opened an office in Florence, Oneida county, N. Y., and in 1872 moved to Pulaski where he has practiced his profession with marked success. For several years past he has made a specialty of the treatment and cure of cancers. In 1891 he erected the handsome, large and commodious dwelling house on the west side of Jefferson Ave. which with his family he now occupies. Dr. Caldwell is a member of the Oswego Co. Medical Society, was its vice president in 1891, and president in 1892; he is also a member of the Oneida Co., Medical Society. In 1872 was a delegate from the Oneida Co.,Society to the annual meeting of the American Medical Society in Washington, D. C. He is also a member of the New York Medical Association and the American Medical Association, and was medical director, Department of New York, Grand Army of the Republic, 1889; United States pension examing surgeon, 1876-'94; coroner of Oswego county from 1876 to 1885, three terms; trustee of the village of Pulaski in 1884 and also served as health officer; commander of J. B. Butler Post, No. 111, Grand Army of the Republic, six years; aide de-camp on commander in chief's staff, 1886 and 1891; is a member of the Masonic fraternity, and of Oswego Lodge, No. 271, Benevolent and Protective Order of Elks.

He is the author of many papers which have been extensively published in the first medical journals of the country.

Dr. Caldwell was married, Oct. 29, 1865, to Miss Carrie E. Griswold, of Florence, N. Y. They have two children, James G. Caldwell, who is connected with an extensive drygoods establishment in Amsterdam, N. Y,, and Henry Williams Caldwell, Jr., a medical student.

G. W. Betts, M. D., began practice in Pulaski in 1880, having on February 17 of that year been graduated at the University of the City of New York and terminating a two years' course of medicine in that institution. James N. Betts, M. D., his father, was a distinguished physician who came to this village in 1854 or '55 and practiced here until he died, in 1892. Dr. G. W. Betts was born in Pulaski October 4, 1858. Upon leaving the village school he first took a course at Ann Arbor, Mich., going thence to New York city to complete his medical education. Upon his return home from school, having in the meantime taken the post graduate course, he entered into practice with his father, the two continuing together until the latter died. In 1881 the doctor was married to Cora Clark, who died in January, 1896. Dr. Betts is earnestly active in all public movements that conserve the interests of the village. He is a member of the Odd Fellows and of the Oswego County Medical Society. The Citizens' Club, the leading social organization of Pulaski business men, is an institution in the welfare of which he is largely interested, and which is successfully directed by him as its president.

J. L. More, M. D., one of the leading physicians of Pulaski, and a regularly employed surgeon for the New York Central railroad, was born in Parish, Oswego county, N. Y., December 20, 1860, and after attending the public schools of that village and Mexico, took a full course in the medical department of the University of New York, from which he was graduated in 1887. Five years earlier, at 22 years of age, he entered the drug store of E. L. Huntington at Mexico, where he had the advantages of a three years' course in practical as well as theoretical pharmacy. Then he began his study of medicine with Dr. S. M. Bennett of Mexico. His first practice was for eight years at Fernwood, thence moving to Pulaski. On August 31, 1887, he married Ella A. Searles, and they have three children—May, 14 years old, Anna, 11, and Jay, 8. Dr. More is

JAMES L. MORE, M. D.

From an Engraving.
JUDGE S. C. HUNTINGTON.

an active member of the leading medical societies, including that of Oswego County, in which he has held the office of President, and the National Medical Association. He has been a member of the Masonic lodge since he was 22 years old and belongs to the Oswego commandery and the Media shrine of Watertown.

Sylvanus Convers Huntington was among the earliest and, for many years, the most prominent member of the Oswego county bar. Possessed of great mental and physical strength, keen and penetrating perceptive power and an indomitable will, together with a broad understanding of criminal law, he made a wide reputation for the skill with which he handled numerous cases that he was called upon to defend. Only one out of sixteen clients he defended, indicted for murder in the first degree, suffered the death penalty, Nathan Orlando Greenfield—a most remarkable record in criminal practice. This was one of the greatest legal contests in the early history of criminal jurisprudence in this state, and on that account deserves mention. Greenfield, charged with the murder of his wife, and to the last insisting that he was innocent, appeared for trial with circumstances greatly against him. For six long years his case dragged through the courts, Judge Huntington, his counsel, alone in defense of his client, battling with the vigor of a giant to secure the verdict of not guilty. Greenfield, when it finally became apparent that he could save his life by pleading guilty in a minor degree, still reiterated his innocence and refused to place himself in any other position. The two ablest criminal prosecutors of the time, ex-District Attorney Lamoree of Oswego and Judge William C. Ruger of Syracuse, were arrayed against Judge Huntington. The latter had become fully convinced that his client was innocent, and he fought for his life as he would have done for his own. Had the law permitted Greenfield's mother to have taken the witness stand, the Judge believed he could have acquitted his client. It was an injustice so apparent that he was afterwards instrumental in

securing an amendment to chapter 182, laws of 1876, which permits persons jointly indicted to testify for each other. In all, the Judge obtained and skillfully conducted three long jury trials, occupying eleven weeks in court in Oswego and Onondaga counties. He made four arguments on appeal, besides twice going before the Governor. It was acknowledged by all who watched the case that never in this state was a better defense made in behalf of a client.

Judge Huntington was born in West Charleston, Vt., April 14, 1820, the sixth child of Joseph and Hannah Convers Huntington, and was the descendant of Simon Huntington of Norwich, Eng., who died aboard ship while coming to this country in 1635. The subject of this sketch was educated at Brownington, Vt., academy and at Oberlin and Dartmouth colleges, and was graduated at the latter in 1845. His schooling was paid for by his own efforts, he having when a boy bought his time of his father. In 1845 he came to Pulaski and studied law with McCarty & Watson and in February, 1846, married Miss Hannah M. Warner of Sandy Creek, his classmate in college, who was responsible for his coming to Pulaski. They spent the following year in Tennessee, he as a tutor in the family of President Jackson at the Hermitage and she as a governess in the family of Mr. Nicholson, President Jackson's adopted daughter. They returned to Pulaski in 1847 and the same year he was admitted to the bar. The two succeeding years he practiced at Belleville, N. Y., and then returned to Pulaski where he resided until his death, which occurred March 2, 1894.

He was county judge in 1856-'60, and was elected district attorney in 1868, but was compelled to resign on account of poor health. Judge Huntington was a careful reader of classics and a thorough student of the sciences, higher mathematics, philosophy and history. His genial nature, good sense and inexhaustible fund of wit and learning made him many friends and genuine admirers. Home life had for him the strongest attractions. His first wife died May 23, 1888, leaving two children, Miss Metelill, who engaged in literary work, and S. C. Huntington, who took

Huested, Photo.
S. C. HUNTINGTON.

IRVING G. HUBBS.

his father's place in the prac ice of law, and is a resident of Pulaski. Both are graduates at Oberlin College. His second wife, Emily L., the daughter of Lavina (Warner) and Benjamin Snow, to whom he was married December 24, 1890, and who is still living, was the widow of Hon. James W. Fenton of Pulaski.

Sylvanus Convers Huntington, son of the late Judge Huntington, succeeded to his father's large law practice upon the death of the latter in 1894, a practice which has steadily grown to become second to that of none other in the town. The management and settlement of estates, straightening out the intricacies of litigated property and Surrogate's practice are the specialties followed by Mr. Huntington in his law work. He is the owner of large tracts of real estate comprising 2,200 acres of dairy farms in the eastern part of the county, to which, however, his law business allows him to give but little personal attention. Naturally a lover of outdoors life and fond of domestic stock, Mr. Huntington enjoys the relief from professional duties that he finds in visiting his several farms and providing for their care. Other duties that his interest in public matters assign to him take up more or less of his time, so that on the whole he is a very busy man. Mr. Huntington was born in Glen Castle, Broome county, N. Y., June 12, 1857, and was prepared for college at the Pulaski Academy, class of 1871.

A studious course at Oberlin terminated in his graduation at that institution at the head of his class in 1876. Then followed a year as teacher of classics in the Pulaski school and the ensuing year in teaching Greek at Oberlin. Then he entered upon a post graduate course at Yale which was cut short by a request from his father who required his services at home, to enter upon the study of law. The next few years found him diligently employed in the Judge's law office at Pulaski, where he pursued his studies and assisted in disposing of a large accumulating business until January, 1882, when he was admitted to practice and was accepted as the junior partner with his father. The firm of S. C. Huntington & Son continued uninterruptedly down to the death of the senior partner. Then he formed a co-partnership with F. G. Whitney which continued six years and was dissolved January 1, 1901. On November 1, 1883, Mr Huntington married Miss Ellen, the daughter of Rev. James and Mary J. Douglas of Pulaski. To them have been born five sons, Carl Douglas, the eldest, George Warner and James Convers (deceased), Maurice Burt and Ralph Isham. Mr. Huntington still occupies the office on Mill street built by his father in 1861, and among his 2,000 law books spends much time in the study of law as a science and its application to the many intricate questions arising in the busy life of today.

Irving G. Hubbs was for six years special county judge of Oswego county, elected for the first time in 1893 and re-elected in 1896. His connection with the Republican party is that of a firm, uncompromising organization man, who has taken a prominent part in county politics, attending caucuses and conventions and otherwise rendering valuable assistance in party counsels as well as contributing to the results of elections by speaking from the platform during successive campaigns. Taking an active part in village matters, his policy is to encourage public improvement and support local enterprise, giving staunch support to the schools and such time as he can spare to his official position as a member of the board of education, which he has occupied

Dunwick, Photo.   IRVING G. HUBBS' RESIDENCE.

Huested, Photo. N. B. SMITH.

two years. Mr. Hubbs has a large law practice to which he is particularly devoted, and which was established by himself comparatively a few years ago—at the time he began practice in the village of Parish, in 1891. Three years later he removed to Pulaski, opening law chambers in the Pulaski National Bank building. While Mr. Hubbs is an indefatigable worker in his profession, still he finds time to identify himself with other important business interests, including a large amount of fire insurance underwriting which is done in his office annually. He is one of the four stockholders in the Charles Tollner's Sons Company, the large manufacturing concern in the village, of which he is the secretary.

He was born in Sandy Creek November 18, 1870, where his father, George L. Hubbs, was a merchant for several years. The family moved to Pulaski a few years later, Mr. Hubbs engaging in the hotel business here and giving his son the advantages of the excellent schools for which Pulaski has long been noted. The latter was graduated at the academy in 1888, and he then took a three years' course at Cornell University where he was graduated in June, 1891, with the degree of L. L. D. In the meantime he pursued the study of law, spending his vacations in the office of the late D. A. King of this village, so that soon after graduation, November 19, 1891, the day after his twenty-first birthday, he was admitted to the bar after an examination held in

Syracuse. He at once began the practice of law at Parish, and it was while there that he married Nannie C., the daughter of W. B. Dixon of Pulaski, the wedding taking place in the latter village January 5, 1893. To them were born two children, Florence Dixon and Marion Elizabeth, the former March 11, 1898, and the latter May 20, 1901. Mr. Hubbs is a member of the Pulaski Chapter and Blue Lodge. His father, who is living in Pulaski, is a veteran of the civil war who at 19 years of age enlisted in the Second Wisconsin Volunteers. After he left the army he came to Sandy Creek, where he married Catharine Snyder. She died in February, 1900.

Nathan B. Smith opened an office for the practice of law in the village of Pulaski on the 4th day of July, 1869, and has since that date continuously occupied offices in the National Bank block, except while district attorney of Oswego county. Mr. Smith is a native of the State of Vermont, and after spending his early boyhood days on his father's farm in Otter Creek Valley, at the age of fourteen entered Burr and Burton Seminary, a famous classical school at Manchester, Vermont. In the year 1863 he graduated from Middlebury College, with the highest honors of his class, and then became connected with the Army of the Potomac and in the Shenandoah Valley as a field correspondent for one of the New York dailies. After returning from the army, Mr. Smith began the study of law in the office of the Hon. John W. Stewart, at Middlebury, afterwards Governor of Vermont, and in the autumn of 1865 came to Pulaski, continuing his legal studies in the office of the late Judge Huntington and also taught classics and higher mathematics in the academy. He was afterward principal for nearly two years, but resigned to complete his professional studies. While a law student, he was elected a Member of Assembly from the Third district of Oswego county and was the youngest member of the Legislature of 1869. Mr. Smith was chosen Special Surrogate of Oswego county in 1875, and in 1881 was elected District Attorney. During his term of office as prosecut-

Huested, Photo. N. B. SMITH'S RESIDENCE.

Huested, Photo.
FREELON J. DAVIS, SPECIAL COUNTY JUDGE.

ing attorney he conducted the trial of Joshua Gifford, who was convicted of murder in the first degree after a memorable trial, lasting four weeks. In the year 1898 he was appointed Referee in Bankruptcy for the District of Oswego county, proving a painstaking and popular judicial officer. Mr. Smith was married on June 3, 1874, to Ellen Grinnell Cornell, youngest daughter of the late Stephen Cornell, who was for many years senior Captain in the U. S. Revenue Service. Two sons were born to them, Cornell N., who is a student in the College of Medicine of Syracuse University, and Walter D., who is a member of the Junior class at Harvard. In all affairs relating to the welfare and advancement of Pulaski, Mr. Smith has taken a deep interest. He has been for many years a member of the Board of Education, and is also a member of the Citizens' Club and other social and civic organizations. Mr. Smith has devoted himself exclusively to the practice of his profession, and in the year 1899 formed a partnership with the Hon. Freelon J. Davis, Special County Judge of Oswego county, and the firm now enjoys an extensive and successful practice.

Hon. Freelon J. Davis, special county judge of Oswego county, a position to which he was elected in 1899 and re-elected in 1902, is one of the active workers in the Republican party of his county, who has been honored by election to important judicial positions and by being selected as a delegate to county, senatorial, congressional and judicial district conventions. In 1896, 1897 and 1898 he occupied important clerkships in the state senate, where he became well informed on legislative matters. Being a steady and indefatigable worker in his chosen profession he has acquired an extended law practice, his office being located in Pulaski. Mr. Davis was born in Orwell, Oswego county, N. Y., October 12, 1867, and is therefore a young man. His father, James F. Davis, and his mother, Amelia A. Stowell, were of New England ancestry. The former practiced dentistry in Orwell and vicinity for the

past fifty years. The early years of Mr. Davis' life were spent in tilling the rough and stony soil of his native town and teaching during the winter months, to acquire means by which to obtain an education. After his graduation at the Sandy Creek academy, in 1887, he took the platform as a party advocate, doing valued service the following year, 1888, in the campaign for Harrison and a protective administration. The succeeding year, at the age of 21, he was elected justice of the peace in the town of Orwell, a position he occupied for eight years—until higher duties called him from home. In 1891 he was elected on the Republican county ticket for Justice of the Sessions and was for several years an associate of Judge Stowell in that court.

Later he took a course in the Albany Law College, graduating from that institution in the spring of 1896, and in the fall of the same year was admitted to the bar as an attorney and counselor at law. Then he returned to his home at Orwell, where for the next three years he practiced his profession, though called away during the sessions of the Legislature. In the spring of 1899 he opened a law office in Pulaski, where he has since been associated with Hon. N. B. Smith in a lucrative and constantly increasing practice.

Mr. Davis is a member of Pulaski Lodge No. 415, F. & A. M.; Pulaski Chapter No. 279, R. A. M.; Welcome Lodge No. 680, I. O. O. F., and Orwell Grange No. 66.

H. R. Huested, the artist who made portraits and views for "Grip's" Historical Souvenirs of Camden, Oneida county, and Pulaski and Mexico, Oswego county, N. Y., is an adept in producing the best modern work in photography. Although a young man he has made rapid advance in the latest and most artistic designs, and has earned a high reputation for the finest grade of negatives and prints. Among his leading styles are Platinums and Artist's Proofs, the former being made to resemble the charcoal drawings of the Sixteenth Century, which are at present thoroughly in line with the Twentieth Century fad for colonial ideas, and the latter presenting a unique

Huested, Photo.
H. R. HUESTED, SOUVENIR ARTIST.

Huested. Photo.   W. H. BROWN.

and exquisite finish, rarely attained outside of city offices.

Mr. Huested operates three galleries—in Camden, Pulaski and Mexico—three progressive, hustling villages. He was born in Adams, Jefferson county, N. Y., May 26, 1874, and his early school comprised terms in that village and Mannsville, Jefferson county, N. Y. Subsequently he finished with a three years' course in Owego academy When 14 years old he engaged with his father, G. P Huested, at Sandy Creek, to learn photography, spending six years under his instruction. Then he was with N. L. Stone at Potsdam, N. Y., and afterwards for a year with his father again. He first began business in his profession at Pulaski, 1897, subsequently opening a gallery at Altmar and afterwards at Orwell. Finally he disposed of the Altmar gallery, and in March, 1899, bought the Camden gallery. In 1901 he sold out the Orwell business, and in June, 1902, bought the Mexico gallery. His three galleries —Camden, Pulaski and Mexico—are completely equipped for all work that is done in photography.

W. H. Brown, who carries on a large hardware and harness store, was born in Pulaski, April 14, 1864. When he was young his parents moved to Mexico where his father, Jacob T. Brown, is still in the harness business, and where he attended school. When he was 26 years old he opened a new harness shop in one of the double stores which are now both required to accommodate his business. A year later he removed into another building and two years afterwards returned to his present location, then taking all of

the room in both stores. Four years ago he bought the block, one of the best business structures in the village. On July 7, 1892, he married Kate, the granddaughter of the well-known pioneer, J. A. Matthewson. Mr. Brown's business is the largest in his several lines in town. He occupies two stores, one 16x50 and the other 24x50, with a shop in the rear. It is a three-story frame structure in thoroughly good order, the second floor occupied by families and the third used by the Maccabees for a lodge room. His business includes all lines kindred to harness and hardware, horse furnishings and bicycles; also sportsmen's goods. Mr. Brown owns a pleasant home in the village, where himself and wife with one son, Stanley, and three daughters, Margaret, Grace and Katherine, live happily.

Jeremiah Angell Matthewson was for more than eighty years a well-known figure in the life of our town. His father, whose full name he bore, was one of the founders of the village and selected its name, erecting the first grist mill, the first hotel or "tavern" and contributing materially to the prosperity of the young community.

The subject of this sketch was born at Hamilton, Madison county, N. Y., September 17, 1805, and died at Pulaski, April 13, 1890. His home was in this village from the age of two years until the end. For many years he was the popular host of the "Pulaski Tavern" on the site of the present Randall House, and proprietor of the "old red mill" immediately south of it. In his early manhood he sailed the great lakes and as captain of the schooner, Pulaski, made a trip to Chicago about the year 1835. The lakes, the rivers, fields and forests were explored by him and in the com-

Dunwick. Photo.   W. H. BROWN'S GENERAL STORE.

From Old Photo.
JEREMIAH A. MATTHEWSON.

panionship of their teeming life he found his keenest pleasures and the subjects for most entertaining stories.

In 1831 he married Elizabeth Hazard. They had two children, Henry, father of Mrs. William H. Brown, of this village, who lived here until his death in 1887; and Sarah, afterwards wife of the late Hon. William G. Adkins, of Oswego, who died in 1884. Their home was the old Matthewson homestead, now the home of Mrs. W. H. Hill, until they built the house now occupied by their granddaughter.

Mr. Matthewson possessed that genial, kindly nature which makes friends and scatters sunshine wherever it is, and a quaint humor which gave spice and zest to his stories of adventure by flood and field. He was an earnest politician whose great pride as such was in the fact that he had voted for every democratic president from Jackson until his death, and the election of village officers was as important to him as that of a president. In early days Mr. and Mrs. Matthewson became commonly known as Uncle Jerry and Aunt Betsey, and as such to almost the entire community, they rounded out their lives in the quiet of old age and sweet content.

Pulaski National Bank—[Concluded—see page 19.]

Then came the change of the following September, already noted, occasioned by the retirement of Charles A. Clark, who died in 1901. His brother, James A. Clark, who retained his own interests in the bank and was in personal charge, after the former's retirement, to the last, died June 13, 1887. The directors held a meeting on the 23d of the same month, and Nellie T. Peck was elected one of their number.

Edward L. Clark died January 18, 1888, and Mrs. Ella M., the wife of Louis J.

Clark, was chosen to fill his place in the board, January 31, 1888.

Mrs. Helen A. Clark died July 22, 1893. On August 2 following (1893) Mrs. Ella M. Clark was elected president and Charles A. Peck was chosen to fill the vacancy on the board of directors. On January 14, 1890, Miss A. S. Klock was made a director in the place of Sherman Clark, jr., and on October 13, 1892, the former was succeeded by Susie H. Peckham, who on October 22, 1894, retired in favor of Willis C. Peck. Mabel A. Clark was elected director July 21, 1896, in the place of Willis C. Peck. On October 20, 1898, Frederick A. Clark succeeded Mabel A. Clark, and on July 3, 1889, he was appointed assistant cashier. Nellie T. and Charles A. Peck resigned April 2, 1900, and were succeeded by Mabel Clark Jones and Jessie Holmes Clark.

The present board of officers and directors, who own all of the stock and all of whom are members of the one family, Mr. and Mrs. Louis J. Clark and their three children, are as follows: President, Mrs. Ella M. Clark; cashier, Mr. Louis J. Clark; assistant cashier, Mr. Frederick A. Clark; Mrs. Mabel Clark Jones and Mrs. Jessie Holmes Clark.

The last financial statement of the bank shows: Capital, $25,000; surplus and undivided profits, $6,000; deposits, $90,000; loans, $73,569; bonds $32,850.

Capt. Ira Doane, who is still living at the advanced age of ninety-five years (in his ninety-sixth), and who is the son of a revolutionary soldier, John Doane, was born June 10, 1807. In May, 1821, his family settled in Orwell and a few years later moved to Pulaski, where he is still living. In 1830 he married Audria Vorce who bore him seven children. Capt. Doane was for many years a farmer, a merchant in Pulaski and a lumberman. He has served with distinction in

From the Democrat.
CAPT. IRA DOANE, OLDEST RESIDENT IN PULASKI.

many public offices, among which are president of the village of Pulaski, collector, jailor and under-sheriff of Oswego county, and inspector of customs in New York city. In his early days he was prominent in the councils of the Democratic party.

John W. Richards, manufacturer of house dresses or wrappers, started manufacturing in that line in the spring of 1891, in company with his father-in-la v, Lucius Jones, with whom he was then engaged in the dry goods business under the

the two stories and basement of the Richards block and the second story of the Betts block. In the beginning four machines answered the purpose but now have twenty machines. The goods are sold direct to the dry goods trade by Mr. Richards and his traveling salesmen, who make periodical trips for that purpose. Two years ago he adopted the stamp of his own production, "J. W. R., Pulaski, N. Y.," which he puts on all of his goods and this he has found to be greatly to his advautage. Mrs. Richards (Elizabeth Addie Jones) to whom he was married

Huested, Photo.
Mrs. J. W. Richards.

J. W. RICHARD'S HOUSE DRESS FACTORY.

Interior of the Factory.

Richards' Residence.

J. W. Richards.

firm name of L. Jones & Co. Their store was located where the factory is now, in the Richards & Betts block. Mr. Jones was one of the older merchants of Pulaski, and was in business here up to the time of his death, Nov. 5, 1894, altogether about forty years. The year after Mr. Jones died the dry goods part of the business was closed out, Mr. Richards since then devoting his entire time to the manufacturing part of it. The plant occupies

April 5, 1882, had considerable experience in her father's store and she assumes a part of the management of the factory, herself and husband working as business partners and sharing the credit for the success the business has enjoyed. Mr. Richards was born on a farm in the town of Richland, Nov. 25, 1854. His father, Dwight Richards was the son of Hiel Richards who came to Richland from Otsego county in the spring of 1818 and who,

W. J. PEACH.

therefore, was one of the early settlers of the town. Mr. Richards' maternal grandfather, John Woodbury, came to the town of Richland in the spring of 1829 and here followed farming for 35 years. In 1864 he moved into the village of Pulaski and went into the grocery business on Salina street near the east end of the bridge. Two or three years later he moved to Orwell where he engaged in trade for about nineteen years, or up to about the time he died, being then at the advanced age of nearly 80 years. J. W. Richards was ten years old when his father moved into the village. After leaving school he was a clerk in R. L. Ingersoll & Co's. bank for about seven and one half years, going from there into business with Mr. Jones. He is a member of the Methodist church, being president of the board of trustees and of the Epworth League. Mr. and Mrs. Richards have two children, Kate Adele and Olive Caroline.

Andrew A. Matthewson was born in Pulaski (the brother of Jeremiah A. Matthewson) and was graduated with honor at Hamilton college. He learned the printer's trade in the Pulaski Banner office under N. Randall and finally purchased the Richland Courier, a sheet afterward merged with the Banner, conducting a book store in connection with his printing office. The store he sold to Silas H. Meacham and the paper to J. C. Hatch. For several years he was on the Rochester papers, afterwards engaging in liter-

ary work, writing novels and short stories. At the age of sixty-six years, August 8, 1882, he died at Lansing, Mich.

W. J. Peach, the President of the village, now at the beginning of his third term of one year each, and who previously served two years as trustee, is a large buyer and shipper of cheese, who secures the best products of the numerous factories in Oneida, Oswego and Jefferson counties and ships them to the principal markets. For the past nineteen years he has been a steady buyer for the prominent cheese and butter house, Alex. W. Grant, of Montreal, with a New York branch, and for some years has also represented E. W. Coon, the large Philadelphia firm, for both of whom he picks up several thousand dollars' worth a year in addition to handling other lots. He is also a dealer in cheese factory supplies for Northern and Central New York.

Mr. Peach is prominently identified with all public interests of Pulaski, taking a deep interest in promoting its growth and trade advantages. He has also been a promoter of such local enterprises as the conditions of the community demanded, being the secretary and a stockholder in the Electric Light Company.

The order of Free Masonry has in him one of its warmest advocates, and he has reached a high standing in that fraternity, being a Shriner and Knight Templer, connected with the Media Temple of Watertown A. A. O. N. M. S., and Lake Ontario Commandery No. 32, K. T., of Oswego, as well as the Pulaski Lodge, F. & A. M., and Pulaski Chapter, R. A. M. Upon the organization of the Citizens Club, he was chosen for its first president, a position he held for three consecutive years. He is one of the active supporters of the First Baptist Church, of which he is a trustee.

Mr. Peach was born in Pulaski, January 20, 1859, and was educated in the academy of that village. His father, William Peach, now living in Pulaski and also active in its public affairs—at the present time a member of the board of trustees —is an Englishman by birth and a resident of this

Dunwick, Photo.   W. J. PEACH'S RESIDENCE.

country since he was twenty-one years old. He was a mason by occupation several years, as well as a builder, and is now sixty-nine years old.

His son when fourteen years old began work in a cheese factory and from that time made that line his special study, being now considered one of the best judges of cheese, and owning the principal interest in a factory. In January, 1892, he married Ellen B. Richardson of Union Square, and in 1897 built a fine residence on Lake street, which is now their home.

W. P. Saunders began trade in Pulaski two years ago by buying out the Thomas Wallis store

Huested, Photo.
SAUNDERS' DEPARTMENT STORE.
Front View.   W. P. Saunders, Manager.
        Interior View.

and opening a department store in all kinds of China and Queen's ware, tinware, silverware, fancy groceries and fruits in their season. This place of business is one of the most attractive and best supplied stores in town. The arrangement of goods is in keeping with the best of the lines with which it is stocked. It is large, well lighted, and has a clean, prosperous appearance. Mr. Saunders lived for a number of years in the west where he met with many interesting experiences. Before oil was discovered at Beaumont, Texas, he

went into that town to buy grazing lands. A year later the tract which he was to have purchased became great oil fields. At the last moment his partner backed out and they missed by the narrowest possible margin an investment yielding untold wealth

Mr. Saunders was born in Canandaigua, N. Y., Sept. 25, 1850. When he was three years old his father died and at the age of fifteen years he went to Kendall, N. Y., to live and attend school. For two years he clerked for De Graff & Griswold in that village and then went to New York where he was a clerk for two years in A. T. Stewart's big store. On Oct. 3, 1871, he married Ida E. Clute, of Port Ontario, N. Y., and locating there erected a building in which he carried on a general store for two years; then for the same period of time he was engaged in business in Kendall, N. Y., and from there he went to Beatrice, Neb., where he resided ten years, occupying the position of teller in the First National Bank. Afterwards he was on the road as a special agent for the Phœnix Insurance Co., of Brooklyn, and for a period of four years was the excursion agent for the Kansas City, Pittsburg & Gulf railroad, his home being in Kansas City. In 1897 he went into the new town of Mena, Ark., and there engaged in the furniture business for a year. Death in his father's family changed his plans and brought him east for permanent location. Mr. Saunders is a member of a western lodge in the Masonic order.

Pulaski Railroad Connections.— A meeting was held to organize the Oswego & Watertown railroad company in the court house at Pulaski, on Jan. 6, 1851. A. Z. McCarty was the chairman. At the next meeting, held on the 13th of the same month the citizens of Richland pledged themselves for one quarter of the stock and to defray the expense of the survey. There arose a spirited discussion as to the route the road should take which continued for some months. In the meantime, at a meeting held in Mexico on Jan. 28, 1851, the articles of incorporation were perfected. Messrs. A. Z. McCarty, Anson R. Jones, George Gurley and Gilbert Woods, of Richland, were included among the directors and the route through Pulaski was adopted. The organization was then called the Oswego Eastern Railroad Co. The directors met with those of the Watertown & Rome road in Pulaski on March 20, to secure, if possible, a combination of the two roads. They could not agree, however.

Another meeting was held in this village, Jan. 1, 1853, to adopt further measures for building the railroad to Oswego and connect it with the proposed road running north to Watertown. Another meeting was held for the same purpose later in the month, a committee from Oswego being present. On the 25th of the same month the directors of the two roads met at Watertown to further promote the scheme. About this time Syracuse began to talk of building a line north from that city (the Syracuse Northern road) to

MRS. E. F. MORRIS.   E. F. MORRIS.

make connections with the Watertown & Rome road at Sandy Creek. The directors of the Oswego & Pulaski road, who at this time were DeWitt C. Littlejohn, John B. Edwards, J. L. McWhorter, Charles Rhodes, A. P. Grant, Jacob Richardson and Joseph C. Wright of Oswego, Robert B. Doxtater of Rome, A. Z. McCarty and Isaac Fellows of Richland, George Marsden of Mexico, Samuel A. Comstock of Albion, and Calvin Seeley of Sandy Creek, met at Oswego, Feb. 3, 1853, and opened subscription books. This was followed by another meeting for the same purpose at Pulaski, Feb. 17, 1853.

Edgar F. Morris, one of the veterans of the war of 1861–'65 now living in Pulaski, who was among the first of Oswego county recruits to respond to the call for defenders of the Union, became a resident of this village in June 1873 and now resides in a pleasant home on North street. Mr. Morris was born in Middleburg, Schoharie county, N. Y., Nov. 22, 1826. Alonzo Morris his father was for some years a tanner and currier in the Schoharie Valley, who when the subject of this sketch was ten years old, in 1836 moved his family to Oswego county and settled on a farm in the town of Palermo. His wife, Nancy was the daughter of Johnathan Joyce, a revolutionary soldier who came to Schoharie county from Cheshire, N. H., where his daughter was born, about 1793. It was at Palermo that Mr. Morris lived his boyhood days

and divided his maturer years up to his enlistment in the Union army between farming and coopering. On March 22, 1849, he married Augustina C., the oldest daughter of the Hon. James J. Coit, of Hastings, Oswego county, a prominent man in the county, a justice of the peace for several years, the supervisor of his town and member of assembly. Mrs. Morris was one of thirteen children, ten of whom are still living, and all of whom received liberal education. Mr. and Mrs. Morris have six children. The eldest is James A. Morris who is engaged in mercantile business at Thousand Island Park where he has carried on trade for several years and who is married to Flora E. Salisbury, of Pulaski. The others, named in order of seniority are Alice, the wife of W. S. Rogers, of Pulaski, Miss Flora Morris, the bookkeeper for her brother at the Islands, Miss Amelia A. Morris, teacher in Porter school at Syracuse for the past eleven years, Edgar Coit Morris, A. M., Professor of English at Syracuse University, and Frank V. Morris, jeweler at Carthage, N. Y., who is married to Jessie Lee Pettis, of Beaver Falls, N. Y.

The beginning of hostilities between the north and the south stirred the patriotism of thousands who were ready at once to offer their lives in the service of their country. Among these was Edgar F. Morris who on Sept. 24, 1861, enlisted as a private in Co. C, 101st N. Y. V. I., which was mustered in at Syracuse and very soon afterwards was sent to the front becoming a part of Birney's brigade, Kearney's division, 3d corps, commanded by Gen. Heintzleman. Mr. Morris was in all of the engagements of his regiment including the second Bull Run where in a charge in which the regiment entered with 700 men, losing all but a hundred, he was so seriously wounded that he was incapacitated for service for about two years. He was one of eight men who rallied around the colors of the regiment and brought them off from the bloody field. The flag is now preserved at Albany. The other engagements in which his regiment was

Dunwick, Photo.   E. F. MORRIS' RESIDENCE.

From Old Photo.
GEORGE W. SEAMANS.

under fire were Whitehouse Landing, Seven Pines, Peach Orchard, Chickahominy, White Oak Swamp, Charles City, Cross Roads, Malvern Hill, Groverton and second Bull Run. Badly hurt by the wound received at the latter engagement, Mr. Morris was taken to the hospital at Portsmouth Grove, R. I., where he was cared for from September until December, 1862, on the 12th of which month he received his discharge and returned home. It was nearly two years later before he was able to return to active service. In September, 1864, he was mustered in with the 184th N. Y. V. I., as first lieutenant in Co. I., with which command he served until it was mustered out at Syracuse July 13, 1865, most of which time, or for about nine months, being on detached duty as adjutant of the regiment and post adjutant on Gen. Joseph B. Carr's staff and for about five or six months assigned to duty as provost marshall. At the close of the war Mr. Morris returned to Palermo where he resided for about a year, from there moving to Cicero, Onondaga county, which was his home for six years, when he moved to Pulaski. For twenty years he was engaged in supervising mason work on public contracts, including the construction of railroads and canal work. Among the contracts on which he was engaged were several on the Erie, Soo Ste Marie and Welland canals. Mr. Morris is a charter member of the J. B. Butler Post, No. 111, G. A. R., of which he is today an active member and in which he has served a term as commander and

three or four years junior vice commander. During all of his life until within the past few years Mr. Morris has been a busy man. Now he and his wife enjoy the latter years of their life in comfort, their children being well situated and prosperous.

George Westcott Seamans became a resident of the town of Albion, Oswego county over sixty years ago, and with the exception of a few years while he was a resident of Adams, Jefferson county, he has been a resident of this county. Most of his life was spent in the town of Albion, near where his father, Royal Seamans, settled when he moved from Richfield, Otsego county, N. Y., early in the forties. Mr. Seamans was born in the town of Richfield, Sept. 9, 1828, and his parents were Royal and Clarritta Seamans. When a boy he cultivated a liking for books and took advantage of every privilege to gain an education. He was a student of the old Mexico Academy and when a young man entered the calling of a teacher and was honored with the office of town superintendent of schools. Mr. Seamans has been a great reader and is well informed in history and literature. He took up the trade of carpenter and builder which has been his employment many years. He was married, Feb. 22, 1855 to Celia Dewey, and the union has been blessed with five children, four of whom, Clayton E., Byron G., Minnie Julia (widow of Willis C. Peck), Mary Clarritta (widow of Henry W. Parker), are living; Ernest Dewey, deceased. In 1864, Mr. Seamans enlisted in the 186th Regiment, N. Y. Vols., in Company C. He went to the front and remained in service with his regiment until the close of the war when he came back to his wife and three small children and occupied the home he left in Albion until about twenty years ago when he removed to this village and became a part owner of a sash, blind and planing mill, which is now known as the Seamans & Mickel mill on Mill street. Mr. Seamans is an ardent believer in the faith of the republican party, a devoted member and officer of the Methodist Episcopal church; past commander and member of J. B. Butler Post, G. A. R.; Pulaski Lodge, No. 415, F. & A. M.

Dunwick, Photo.   GEORGE W. SEAMANS' RESIDENCE.

Dunwick, Photo. B. G. SEAMANS.

Byron George Seamans was born in the town of Albion, Seamans District, N. Y., May 22, 1862. Resided with his parents, Mr. and Mrs. G. W. Seamans until fourteen years of age, when he went into the world to make his own destiny. From a farm hand to an apprentice at milling, later a student and teacher in the Sandy Creek High School and the school on the Ridge Road, then apprentice in the office of the Sandy Creek News and in 1884 editor and proprietor of the Copenhagen News at Copenhagen, N. Y., and gaining other newspaper experience as editor and proprietor of the Carthage Leader, associate on the staff of the Watertown Herald. In April, 1885, Mr. Seamans became half owner of the Richfield Springs Mercury and in 1886 the firm established the Richfield Springs Daily. In 1895 he purchased the Pulaski Democrat, which is still in his possession. In politics Mr. Seamans is a republican and served the county of Otsego as clerk of the board of supervisors and in Oswego county he has been identified with the party as publisher of a republican paper and an active worker in town and county politics. He is prominently connected with church and social organizations, being a member of the Congregational church, a member of Pulaski Lodge, F. & A. M.; Pulaski Chapter, R. A. M.; Pulaski Chapter, O. E. S.; A. S. Warner Camp, S. of V.; Pulaski Grange; Pulaski Lodge, A. O. U. W.; Seamans Association, P. of I. Mr. Seamans married Mrs. Ella Caswell Hull, December, 1886. The fruit of the union has been three daughters, two of whom, Ruth Ella and Nina May—twins aged twelve years—are living, Julia, deceased. Mrs. Seamans has one son, George Daniel Hull, aged eighteen.

Early Business Men.—Those in Pulaski about 1844-8 were the following:—Attorneys, C. & J. A. Rhodes, A. Z. McCarty, John B. Watson, Sykes & Mathewson, Daniel McCarty and J. T. Stevens; Physicians, Hiram Murdock, John M. Watson, J. V. Kendall, George O. Gilbert and H. F. Noyes; General Merchants, G. W. Fuller, D. H. Fisk, Wardwell and Stillman, E. M. Hill, Samuel Hale, J. A. Clark, Frey Lane, Jones & Angell and N. M. Wardwell; Blacksmiths, Allen Crandall, John Jones, John Box Jr. and Robbins; Wagon Shop, John David and Charles G. Hinman; Tanner and Leather Manufacturer, Dewey C. Salisbury; Livery Stable, Barney Peck; Milliner, Mrs. Fisk, Miss W. A. Gilbert and Mrs. E. Way: Tailors, Henry Mitchell, Edward S. Salisbury, William S. Carpenter, successor to E. S. Salisbury, and Wm. June; Woolen Manufacturers, Stearns & West; Harness Makers, Sidney M. Tucker and A. C. Burton; Hat Manufacturers, Jacob Smith, A. H. Stevens and Henry Emerson; Paper Mill, Tallmadge, Wright & Co.; Eagle Furnace, Plow and Stove Manufacturers, Snow & Dodge; Engineer and Surveyor, Charles H. Cross; Painters, D. S. Robinson and L. B. Rice; Jeweler, A. A. Mathewson; Stoves and Hardware, Meacham & Crandall and L. B. Norton; Machinists, R. B. Boynton and Benjamin Dow; Sash and Blinds, Lafayette Alfred; Carriage Works, Ingersoll & Osgood; Empire Machine Shop, Albert Maltby; Eagle Oil Mill, G. B. Griffin, succeeded by A. B. Collins and A. M. Duncan.

The Postmasters.—The postoffice in Pulaski was established in 1817 and was called Richland. Henry White, the first postmaster, was succeeded the following year by Orville Morrison. Then came Hiram Hubbell in 1819. Other postmasters, so far as can be learned, were Daniel H. Fisk in 1842, Henry N. Wright in 1844, Joseph T. Stevens in 1849, Benjamin Rhodes in 1851 and Newell

Dunwick, Photo. B. G. SEAMANS' RESIDENCE.

Huested, Photo.

PULASKI DEMOCRAT—EDITOR AND STAFF OF EMPLOYES.

1, Miss Lena Pierce, Compositor; 2, Harry W. Smith, Pressman; 3, Robert V. Davis, Advertising Compositor; 4, Frank Brennan, Compositor; 5, Mrs. Ritta Parker, Bookkeeper; 6, T. W. Shaul, Assistant Editor; 7, Miss Mary Richardson, Compositor; 8, B. G. Seamans, Editor and Proprietor; 9, Miss Pearl Goodrich, Compositor; 10, C. L. Finster, Foreman; 11, Harry Klock, Apprentice.

Wright in 1852. On January 27, 1853, the name of the postoffice was changed to Pulaski by the request of Newell Wright, who was then postmaster. On January 14, 1854, William C. Hemstead was appointed. He was followed by Henry C. Wright in 1856, who was again appointed in 1866, and John B. Watson who received the appointment in 1861 and 1867. In 1871 it was made a presidential office and Mr. Watson was again appointed. After him came John T. McCarty followed by Don C. Bishop, who had a short term when he was succeeded by Lawson R. Muzzy. Don C. Bishop was again appointed. He was succeeded in 1897 by R. W. Box, the present postmaster.

The Newspapers of Pulaski.—The Banner was the first paper published in the county outside of Oswego. It was published by Nathan Randall until 1832, when he sold it to A. A. Matthewson and G. G. Foster, who disposed of it in 1833 to James Gedd. The latter suspended publication in 1835. In 1836 Daniel Ayer purchased the material and began publishing the Pulaski Advocate which he sold in 1838 to a Mr.

Dickenson, who at that time owned the Port Ontario Aurora. He consolidated the two under the name of the Pulaski Advocate and Aurora, and early in 1840 sold out to Daniel Ayer, who discarded the last name and published the Advocate until 1842 when it was discontinued. In 1843 William H. S. Winans established the Pulaski Courier and on Feb. 25, 1847, sold it to A. A. Matthewson, who changed the name to the Richland Courier and continued the publication until Sept. 25, 1850, when he sold it to Joseph C. Hatch, who changed its name to the Northern Democrat. On July 21, 1853, he sold out to Beman Brockway who was subsequently the founder and editor of the Watertown Times. Under him the name was changed to the Pulaski Democrat, under which name it has since been successfully conducted. Mr. Hatch again took charge of the paper Dec. 8, 1853, and in 1855 was succeeded by Stephen C. Miller and Don A. King. Prof. Miller died in November, 1869, and the business passed into the possession of Lawson Reade Muzzy, who in January, 1894, enlarged it. The Democrat originally advocated the principles of the democratic party, but was changed to an independent sheet in 1869. In the great fire of October, 1881, it was burned

From the Democrat.   HOME OF THE PULASKI DEMOCRAT.

BENJAMIN SNOW. (Huested)   MRS. BENJAMIN SNOW. (Dunwick)
JOHN BACON WATSON. (Copied from Old Photo)
JOHN BENJAMIN SNOW. (Huested)   NORMAN WATSON SNOW.
(From Old Photo)

prentice twenty years ago. He has applied himself to the trade with great diligence until he is without a superior in the printer's art. Theodore W. Shaul, assistant editor and pressman, has had an experience of sixteen years in printing and newspaper work and has been in the Democrat office over six years. He is an able assistant and fills his important position with marked success.

John B. Watson was born in Trenton, Oneida county, April 17, 1817. He came to this village with his father when only fourteen years of age. He was a student at Belleville Union Academy, N. Y., and there formed a friendship with Judge Joseph Mullen that was continued throughout their lives. He was a diligent student of refined tastes and wide culture and remained such throughout his life. He selected the law as the profession most congenial to his tastes and entered the office of Hon. A. Z. McCarty as a student, subsequently becoming his law partner. In 1845 he was elected Justice of the Peace and continued to hold that office to the date of his death. He was appointed postmaster in 1861 and held that office continuously until his decease. In 1843 he was married to Lydia E. Wood, a sister of the late General D. P. Wood of Syracuse. She died July 6, 1853. Four children were born to them, of whom two survive, Mrs. Benjamin Snow, of this village and Mrs. Wesley E. Bates of Kirkwood, Mo. His second wife was Mrs. Anna E. Cole, to whom he was married in the year 1856 and to whom two children were born, one only surviving, Mrs. Nathan A. Caldwell, of Hagaman, N. Y. His entire life was characterized by conscienteousness

out but its enterprising publisher the next morning published an extra from one of the churches. Mr. Muzzy continued the ownership of the Democrat until 1895, when it passed into the hands of its present owner, Byron G. Seamans. The fiftieth anniversary of the paper was celebrated in 1900 by the publication of a double sheet on fine book paper. The edition was full of local history and illustrations. In September, 1901, at the opening of Vol. LII of the Democrat, the plant was moved to a new block built especially for it, at the corner of Broad and Park streets, and the facilities of the office greatly augmented. A new press was placed in the office and the paper changed from the old style, four page, to the modern eight page paper with seven columns to the page. The change has been greatly appreciated, as is evidenced by increased circulation and increased advertising patronage. The office is equipped with three power presses and a folding machine. It has an abundance of the latest type faces and enjoys a large business in book and commercial printing. A force of ten persons in the office and one solicitor and collector outside is employed. Clifford L. Finster, foreman, entered the office as ap-

Dunwick, Photo.   BENJAMIN SNOW'S RESIDENCE.

A. E. OLMSTEAD.   MRS. A. E. OLMSTEAD.
ORIMELL B. OLMSTEAD.   FRED L. OLMSTEAD.

and fidelity to duty. He died October 7, 1880, aged sixty-three years.

Benjamin Snow was born in Springfield, Mass. February 8, 1800. At an early age he learned the trade of gunsmith at the U. S. arsenel at Watervliet. N. Y., and entered a shop at Rome, N. Y., where he remained until 1821, when he came to Pulaski, where he opened a shop and made and repaired guns. On February 10,

1825, he married Miss Lovina Warner, of Clinton, Oneida county, N. Y., and this union was blessed with five sons and one daughter, three of whom survive: Norman G. Snow of La Salle, Ill; Benjamin Snow of Pulaski, and Mrs. Emily Huntington of New York city. Mr. Snow followed his trade until 1832, when in company with William Greenwood, he founded what is now known as the Ontario Iron Works of this village. Mr. Snow, highly respected as a citizen, was honored by his selection as an officer of the town and president of the village. He was one of the constituent members of the First Baptist church and one of its most loyal supporters up to the time of his death, which occured in 1848.

Benjamin Snow, son of Benjamin and Lovina Snow, was born in Pulaski, May 30th, 1834. Mr. Snow received his education in the schools of Pulaski and Clinton, N. Y., after which he entered the foundry founded by his father in this village. In 1867 he married Miss Mary M. Watson, daughter of John B. Watson. Two children have been born to Mr. and Mrs. Snow, Norman W. and John B. Norman was educated at the Pulaski school and Colgate academy at Hamilton. Then he went to Kansas and later to Denver where he took a commercial course at Woodworth's College. Upon his gradnation he entered the Union bank of Denver and was there stricken with typhoid fever. Norman was a young man of excellent Christian character and was prominent in Church work. At the time of his death he was but twenty-two years of age. Benjamin Snow is superintendent of the Ontario Iron Works and is one of Pulaski's most highly respected citizens. At twenty-two years of age he united with the Masonic lodge and was elected Master. For more than thirty-six years he has served as secretary of the Lodge. Mr. Snow is interested in all good causes and is known as a loyal citizen and a faithful supporter of the church

Messenger, Photo.   A. E. OLMSTEAD'S RESIDENCE AND STORE, ORWELL. N. Y.

of which his father was a constituent member, the First Baptist. Mr. Snow has been an officer in this church over twenty years. He also served as secretary of the local school board twenty years. John B. Snow is a young man of excellent character and great promise. Having graduated from Pulaski Academy and taken a course at Mount Hermon school, he prepared for college and entered New York University this fall.

Arthur E. Olmstead was born at Orwell, June 20, 1850. His father, Orimell B. Olmstead, commenced the mercantile business at Orwell in 1840. In the year 1874, Arthur E. succeeded his father in the store. In 1876 he married Ida J. Davis, of Clinton, Michigan. In 1883 he built a brick store 35x101 feet on the old site where his father commenced business. This is where he is carrying on business at the present time. He has two sons,

of the village when Surveyor Wright with tripod and compass, located the lines. The first firm operated the works about five years and was succeeded by Snow, Brown & Simmons. After five years, this in turn was succeeded by Snow & Thomas, who remained in control two years and was followed by Snow & Dodge for four years. At this time Snow & Fisher assumed control, which they held a portion of one year to the date of the death of the senior member of the firm which occurred Nov. 4, 1848. Norman G. Snow, eldest son of Benjamin Snow, sr., with Fisher & Osgood, conducted the works till the spring of 1849, at which time Norman G. Snow assumed control and operated the plant till the year 1854, when Fisher & Wood became owners of the property. In the year 1856 this firm was succeeded by Fisher & Ling, who conducted it for about thirty years. This firm enlarged the main building, erected a convenient foundry and greatly in-

Dunwick, Photo. THE ONTARIO IRON WORKS, PULASKI, A. E. OLMSTEAD, ORWELL, N. Y., Proprietor.
Residence owned by A. E. Olmstead and occupied by Herman Killiam, Foreman of the Machine Shop.
The Foundry.   The Machine Shop.

Orimell B., born Oct. 16, 1880, and Fred L., born Nov. 19, 1881.

Besides conducting the store at Orwell and the Ontario Iron Works at Pulaski, he is heavily interested in farming, having 1,400 acres of farming land in the towns of Orwell and Richland, also a cheese factory at Orwell village.

The Ontario Iron Works were founded in the year 1832 by Benjamin Snow, sr., and William Greenwood. Benjamin Wright, a surveyor and owner of about 300 acres of land within the village limits, donated the land whereon the main building of the works was erected. This was done with the provision "That a two-story stone structure, 40x60 feet in dimensions, and lying due north and south, should be constructed." Considerable interest was manifested by the residents

creased the business. In the year 1886 the firm Averill & Sharp became the owners and retained possession until July, 1892, when Arthur E. Olmstead, of Orwell, N. Y., purchased the property and promptly commenced the work of repairing the buildings and replacing the old machinery with the most modern makes. Skillful men were employed and the manufacture of a superior make of portable engines and boilers for the New England market was inaugurated. Charles A. Kinney, of Meriden, Conn., general agent, by his exceptional ability as manager and salesman, created so vigorous a market for this product that an addition to the machine shop became necessary. A two-story brick building, 53x70 feet in dimensions was accordingly built in the year 1901. With this addition it is now running with extended equipment and forms one of the most complete

Dunwick, Photo. A. E. OLMSTEAD AND STAFF OF EMPLOYES.

Standing (from left to right)—C. L. Bonney, George E. Buck, F. A. Prouty, C. A. Sackett, Lyman Mallory, Frank Brundage, Frank E. Gurley, Clarence Kelsey, G. E. Wallace. Seated (from left to right)—F. J. Weeks, H. S. Killam, Foreman, A. E. Olmstead, Proprietor, Benjamin Snow, Superintendent, Henry Filkins, F. P. Hardy.

plants in this vicinity. The engines and boilers are absolutely safe in operation. The utmost precaution is used in the selection of all materials entering into their construction and the most pronounced satisfaction is expressed by the purchaser and operator. The proprietor has the confidence of the community, who admire his energy, his business ability and progressiveness and they justly expect that an increasing and profitable business will amply reward him.

The Congregational Church of Pulaski was incorporated on Jan. 22, 1811, as the First Congregational Church and Society of Richland. The articles of incorporation were filed in the clerk's office of Oneida county, which then included the greater portion of the territory now Oswego county. At a meeting of all the male inhabitants of the town who were interested in the legal organization of the church held at the house of John Meacham on the 25th of February, 1811, articles of agreement were signed and the following persons were chosen trustees: Erastus Kellogg, John Meacham, Silas Harmon, Timothy Maltby, Rufus Price, Simon Meacham and Moses R. Porter. Robert G. Rowe was appointed clerk of the trustees. At a subsequent meeting held November 25, 1811 additional articles were adopted which provided that payments for the support of the pastor be made to the trustees, one-third in money and two-thirds in produce, and that the minister, Rev. Oliver Leavitt, should preach half the time at the settlement by the river, where the village is now located and the other half of the time in the settlement by Captain Isaac Meacham's. Prior to such legal organization a religous society had existed for about three years which held meetings occasionaly at the homes of some of the early settlers. This society was an offshoot or branch of the Congregational church at Pawlet, Vt., and as its founders were closely associated with the early settlement and development of the town, a reference to them is of interest.

In the year 1805 a little company of men consisting of Ephraim Brewster, Gershom Hale, John Meacham, Simon Meacham, Philo Sage and David Kidder came from Pawlet, Vt., to establish a settlement in this region and reached the present site of Pulaski on the Salmon river on the 22nd. of March, 1805, and found here only one log cabin, owned by Benjamin Winch, a surveyor. (See "History of Pulaski" for more about them.)

In 1807, when Thaddeus Harmon and Levi Meacham were about to join these early settlers, the Congregational church at Pawlet, Vt., of which the Rev. John Griswold was pastor, constituted them with five others, a branch church. During the same year Joel Harmon came to the new settlement and was earnest in his efforts to establish more permanently the institutions of religion.

THE EPISCOPAL CHURCH.

REV. JESSIE B. FELT.

In the autumn of this year the little church was more fully organized at his house by the adoption of articles of faith and a covenant, which were signed by the following persons: Thaddeus Harmon, John Meacham, Levi Meacham, Joel Harmon, Simon Meacham, Lucy Meacham, Olive Hale, Polly Meacham and Ruth Harmon.

Rev. David Spear, of Rodman, N. Y., was present at this meeting and administered the sacrament of the Lord's Supper, and thereafter regular Sabbath worship was maintained with the reading of sermons and services conducted by Messrs. Lassell and Reddell, missionaries from Vermont, who occasionally visited the little colony until the year 1811, when the church was legally incorporated as above mentioned. The influence of this missionary church upon the character of the early settlers was shown by the remarkable fact, that when the first subscription list of the society was signed, it contained the names of eighty-four men, whose pledges varied from fifty cents to ten dollars.

On the 25th of December, 1811, Rev. Oliver Leavitt was installed as first pastor of the church. Mr. Leavitt's ministry continued for about eight years, and was very successful. Forty-seven persons united with the church as the fruit of a revival in 1814–15. In the year 1811, the society received a gift of fifty acres of land from Col. Clark, of Pawlet, Vt., who afterward donated the land upon which the first house of worship was erected. The congregation continued to worship in private homes, in the old log school house that stood near the present site of the Baptist church and the court house, until 1829 when a commodious edifice was erected on Church street.

The first parsonage was built on land near the present cemetery and was used as a pastor's residence until the year 1856 when a new parsonage was purchased on Bridge street. The first church edifice was used for religious purposes until 1865 when the corner stone for the present commodious house of worship was laid at the corner of Lake avenue and Church street during the pastorate of Rev. James Douglas. This fine, brick church,

which is a fitting memorial of the pastorate of Dr. Douglas, one of the longest and ablest in the history of the society, was dedicated on the 24th of April 1867 and the parsonage used at the present time was purchased in 1884. After the resignation of the Rev. Oliver Leavitt the church was without a pastor for nearly two years. Rev. Oliver Ayre was installed as pastor in Feb. 1822 and continued his labors for five years. During his pastorate 77 additions were made to the church members. Rev. George Freeman was pastor of the church from Dec. 1827 to Jan 1830. During this period the first church edifice was erected and 28 persons united with the church. In March 1830 Rev. Ralph Robinson became pastor. His pastorate which continued until Jan. 1846 was one of the most notable in the history of the church. He was a man of strong convictions, rigid in doctrine and a most successful and earnest pastor. During his pastorate there were several revivals and 215 names were added to the roll of members. He was succeeded by the Rev. Thomas Salmon, installed as pastor, August, 1846, whose pastorate is now affectionately remembered by some of the older inhabitants of the town. His sketch is published more fully on another page. Rev. Fayette Shepard was pastor of the church from May 1855 to April 1858, and during that period 46 additions were made to the membership. He was succeeded by the Rev. Lucian W. Cheney who served as its pastor until Nov. 1864. During this time 41 persons united with the church. The Rev. James Douglas accepted a call to the church in Dec. 1864. His pastorate continued until Jan. 1883 and was the longest and most notable in the church history. He was a graduate of Hamilton College and Auburn Theological Seminary. He was professor of Greek in Genesee College, now Syracuse University, and was pastor of the Congregational church of Rutland, N. Y. For eleven years after his resignation he was a lecturer in

Dunwick, Photo. [See Sketch p. 40.]
THE CONGREGATIONAL CHURCH.

From the Democrat.   THE OLDEST RESIDENCE IN PULASKI.

The First Baptist Church.—Among the early settlers of the town of Richland were several Baptist families, but no regular meetings were held by them in Pulaski until the year 1824 or 1825. Then a Deacon Templeton, of Sandy Creek, came and conducted prayer and conference meetings in the Court House and in private residences. In the year 1826, the services of Rev. Norman Guiteau, a man of culture and a strong preacher, were secured, but the budding hopes of his usefulness here were quickly blasted by his sudden death. His place was filled in due time by the Rev. Jason Lothrop, under whose labors the little band of some twenty members increased to about twenty-eight members. Pursuant to the call of May 17, 1828, the following representatives met in the Court House on the 9th day of June, following, to consider the expediency of organizing a church: from the Baptist church at Richland, Revs. Ferris and Holmes with N. Powers, J. Holmes and Mr. Bangs; from the Baptist church at New Haven, Rev. R. T. Smith, with Barzillai Snow, John Gratton and Cyrus Severance; from the Baptist church at Ellisburg, Rev. Timothy Brewster, with B. Freeman; from the Baptist church at Sandy Creek, Thomas Gratton, Calvin

Oberlin Theological Seminary, where he died in 1891. He was a man of deep learning, a forceful preacher, and a profound thinker. During his pastorate of eighteen years 120 members were added to the church and his memory is now revered by the present generation as well as by the older people of the town. Rev. Albert Kinnmuth was pastor from Jan. 1884 to March 1886 and 17 additions were made to the church membership. Rev. A. H. Post was pastor of the church for three years from Jan. 1887 to Jan. 1890 and eight united with the church. Rev. A. N. Raven succeeded from 1890 to Oct. 1892 and twelve additions were made. Rev. Abram S. Emmons was pastor from Dec. 1892 to May 1898 and as a result of his pastoral labors 34 names were added to the church roll of membership. The present pastor Rev. Jesse B. Felt entered upon his duties in Dec. 1898. During his pastorate many improvements have been made in the parsonage and in the interior of the house of worship. Thirty-four have been received into church fellowship. Since its organization 784 have become members of the church and its present membership comprises 133 on the active list besides 28 non-resident members.

The Sunday school which was organized in 1817 has an enrollment in the main school of 114 and in the home department of 60. It is well equipped with modern appliances and is doing satisfactory work. The following are the officers: Superintendant, Jesse B. Felt; associate superintendant, Louis J. Clark; superintendant of the home department, Mrs. Ella K. Wright; secretary, Miss Marion E. Wright; treasurer, Miss Nellie Fitch; librarian, Miss Lizzie Fuller; organist, Mrs. Jessie M. Greene; chorister, Miss L. Grace Henderson.

The officers of the church and society are as follows: Deacons, Z. R. Evans, George W. Douglas and Byron G. Seamans; deaconesses, Miss Lizzie Fuller, Mrs. W. H. Austin and Mrs. Ella M. Wright; clerk, N. B. Smith; treasurer, Z. R. Evans. Trustees, H. B. Clark, G. W. Douglas, B. G. Seamans, T. S. Meacham and N. B. Smith; clerk, S. C. Huntington; treasurer, Z. R. Evans.

From Old Photo.
THE OLD BAPTIST CHURCH.

REV. J. FOSTER WILCOX.

Murray and Jedediah Gratton. The conference appointed as its representatives, Rev. Jason Lothrop, T. C. Baker, Benjamin Snow and Horace Phillips. The following were also present and were invited to participate in the labors of the council: Rev. Gamaliel Barnes, John and William Manwarring, Mexico; H. B. Rounds and David Carlisle, Newport. Rev. Jason Lothrop was chosen moderator, and T. C. Baker, clerk of the council. After due deliberation it was voted to recommend the organization of a local church, and on this day the First Baptist church, of Pulaski was formed. The service of recognition was one of great interest. The Rev. R. T. Smith, of New Haven, preached the sermon, taking for his text, "Fear not, little flock; for it is your Father's good pleasure to give you the kingdom," —Luke xii, 32. Rev. Mr. Ferris, of Richland, gave the hand of fellowship, and the Rev. Timothy Brewster gave the address to the members. T. C. Baker was selected to act as church clerk. On the 12th day of July, Benjamin Snow (father of our present beloved Deacon Benjamin Snow) and T. C. Baker were elected deacons. At this time there were twenty-six constituent members, viz: Rev. Jason Lothrop, Benjamin Snow, T. C. Baker, R. Clyne, Eli Green, Horace Phillips, John Hendrickson, Sylvester Hills, Oliver Allen, Mrs. Allen and daughter, Sibyl S. Baker, Lovina Snow, Delia Doane, Betsy Jones, Polly Hendrickson, Charlotte May, Amanda Weed, Susan Phillips, Lovina, Meacham, Ann Fellows, Cynthia Bass, Eliza Bragdon and Fanny Manwarring. The church

united with the Black River Association and remained a member for about five years, when the Oswego Baptist Association was organized, and then united with the county organization. Rev. Jesse Elliot followed Rev. Lothrop as pastor and labored very acceptably and successfully for nearly four years, preaching in the Court House every other Sunday, supplying the First Richland church one half of the time and proclaiming the Gospel in barns, dwellings and school houses in different parts of the town. Those years, 1830-31-32 and onward were times of great refreshing. Two and three days' meetings began to be held. Christians went forth two by two praying with the scattered inhabitants of the township. Conversions were frequent and many were baptized. The church immediately resolved itself into a missionary, then a tract and soon afterward into a Sunday School society. On the 31st day of August, 1829, T. C. Baker, Eli Weed, Hiram Hubbell, Issac H. Sterns, Wm. Hale, Jos. Avery and Robert Clyne were named as the building committee, who proceeded to purchase a lot and erect a meeting house which was finished and in December 1834, dedicated to the worship of Almighty God. The day and preacher of the sermon are not recorded. When the frame was raised the Rev. Jesse Elliot offered prayer. Several years later, under the pastorate of the Rev. S. J. Decker, the building was enlarged and repaired. This enlargement is supposed to have occurred in 1859, and at the re-dedication which probably occurred in the winter of 1859-60, Rev. A. Cleghorn, pastor of the Baptist church at Belleville, delivered the sermon. The church was again rebuilt in 1894 under the pastorate of Rev. D. J. Bailey and re-dedicated on the 23d of May, 1895. The members of the church and congregation revealed their loyalty and love by giving liberally and cheerfully to dedicate the building free from debt, and the beautiful and modern building in which we worship to-day was erected by the great sacrifice of the members.

Dunwick, Photo. THE FIRST BAPTIST CHURCH.

JUNIOR LEAGUE OF CHRISTIAN ENDEAVOR, M. E. CHURCH.
1, Althea Orton, 2, Clara West, 3, Florence Frary, 4, Albert Bean, 5, Flossie Macy, 6, Frank Maxwell, President; 7, Edith Scriber, 8, Beulah Dillenbeck, 9, Irene Darling, 10, Kate Richards, Treasurer; 11, Lyle North, 12, Mrs. Richards, Superintendent; 13, Olive Richards, 14, Florence Herrick, 15, Harold Mallon, 16, Grace Utley, 17, Orlene Darling, 18, Jay Darling, 19, Mae Pride, 20, Fred Haggerty, 21, Flora Decatur, 22, Clayton Parker, 23, Ernest Dillenbeck.

The EpworthLeague Methodist Episcopal church. The young people of this church were organized into a Christian Endeavor society in the autumn of 1888, during the pastorate of Rev. Alexander Bramley, Mrs. Helen Bramley being the first president. At a meeting of this society held Sept. 20, 1898, during the pastorate of Rev. Charles H. Guile, the Epworth League was organized. On Sept. 30, the following officers were elected: President, S. R. Trumbull; first vice-president, Miss Frances Ehle; second vice-president, Mrs. W. S. Rogers; third vice-president, Miss Hattie Hollis; fourth vice president, Miss Bertha Holmes; secretary, Miss M. J. Bean; treasurer, David Mahaffy.

The dedicatory sermon was delivered by the Rev. W. H. Maynard D. D., of Colgate University, and the evening address was given by the Rev. F. L. Anderson, D. D., of Rochester. Since the organization of the church, the following named brethren have served it as pastors in the order named: Jason Lothrop, R. T. Smith, Jesse Elliot, I. N. T. Tucker, C. B. Taylor, Abner Webb, M. V. Wilson, George A. Ames, M. B. Comfort, J. J. Townsend, D. D. Owen, I. N. Steelman, D. J. Bailey and J. Foster Wilcox, the present pastor. The average pastorates have been about four years, but some have largely exceeded that length. The early position of the church on the subject of temperance is deserving of notice. On the 20th of June, 1829, the following record was made: "Voted unanimously that this church do hereby resolve that each and every member refrain from the use of ardent spirits in any case except as medicine." The membership, 215, is the largest at present it has ever been. The church is known as "The church of the cordial welcome."

The officers of the church are as follows: Pastor, Rev. J. Foster Wilcox; clerk, Benjamin Snow; treasurer, Clifford L. Finster; deacons, Benjamin Snow, Frank E. McChesney, Marshall B. Lighthall, Ephraim M. Averill; trustees, Albert F. Betts, James H. Betts, Frank B. Rickard, William J. Peach, M. B. Lighthall, John W. Bonney; Sunday school superintendent, J. L. Hutchens.

In January following the change in the name and character of the society, there were forty-five active members enrolled. The annual meeting of the League for the election of officers for the ensuing year was held in the chapel on Wednesday evening, April 2, 1902, when the following were elected: President, J. W. Richards; first vice president, Miss Frances Ehle; second vice president, Miss Carrie Wood; third vice president, Miss Rose Fenton; fourth vice president, Miss Kate Haggerty; secretary, Miss Ina B. Austin; treasurer, Walter Erskine. Superintendent of the Junior League, Mrs. J. W. Richards.

The Woman's Christian Temperance Union of Pulaski, was organized on the 31st of July, 1888, Mrs. G. M. Gardinier assisting in the organization. The first officers chosen were Mrs. Bram-

THE WOMAN'S CHRISTIAN TEMPERANCE UNION.
1, Mrs. J. Foster Wilcox, 2d Vice-President; 2, Mrs. M. M. Pratt, Assistant Secretary; 3, Mrs. Ann J. Richards, Past Secretary; 4, Mrs. F. G. Utley, Secretary; 5, Mrs. Lora Prouty, Treasurer; 6, Mrs. Alta M. Austin, Past President; 7, Mrs. Albert Hough, Corresponding Secretary; 8, Mrs. Z. R. Evans, 3d Vice President; 9, Mrs. Benjamin Snow, President; 10, Mrs. Sidney O. Barnes, 1st Vice-President.

REV. SIDNEY O. BARNES.

ley, president, Mrs. Owen and Mrs. Post, vice-presidents, Mrs. A. A. Maltby, secretary, and Mrs. Benjamin Snow, treasurer. Our meetings were held semi-monthly in the churches alternately. We afterwards rented the hall over Mr. Hollis' store. Subsequently we occupied the hall over O. V. Davis' store, and later the one owned by Albert Austin. We finally gave up our rooms and met monthly at the homes of the members.

The second year of our existence we sent petitions to all the voters whose names we could obtain, requesting them to vote for no-license. We also served dinner in the court house on election day, to all the voters. That year the no-license votes prevailed. The next year we pursued the same course, but speeches had been made by those in favor of license, showing that taxes would be increased if there was no license money to use, and although we made a careful estimate of the amount of increase, showing that it would be the merest trifle for the average tax payer, the majority of the voters wanted license.

After that year we could not serve dinners at the court house because a law had been passed prohibiting electioneering near the polls, and the dinner was doubtless considered a powerful, though silent pleader, but we did what we could to satisfy the demand for food and drink with harmless viands, serving coffee and lunch in cases of fires, to firemen and others. Only four of the original members remain with us. Some have moved away and some have been promoted to a spiritual existence. The last promotion was that of Mrs. A. A. Maltby, who was one of the first and most efficient workers in the cause of temperance, having filled successfully nearly every office in the local union as also the presidency in the county union. Four of the original members are Mrs. Douglas, who as well as her husband, Rev. James Douglas, was among the earliest and most energetic laborers for the promotion of temperance; Mrs. Ann Richards also one of the early and late workers, who was both recording and corresponding secretary eight consecutive years; and Mrs. B. Snow, and Mrs. Alta Austin, who, though among the first burden bearers in the field, are yet in the prime of life. The following persons have served as presidents: Mrs. Bramley, Mrs. Willis Peck, Mrs. W. H. Austin, Mrs. A. A. Maltby, Mrs. W. Holmes, Mrs. F. G. Utley, Mrs. B. Snow. The society now numbers forty-five active members. The officers at the present time are: President, Mrs. Snow; vice presidents, Mrs. Barnes, Mrs. Wilcox, Mrs. Evans; corresponding secretary, Mrs. Hough; recording secretary, Mrs. Utley; treasurer, Mrs. Prouty.

The First Methodist Episcopal Church.—According to early reports, the Methodist Episcopal church first began its work in this vicinity in 1811, meeting for a time in the bar room of Pliny Jones' hotel, one mile from the village toward Syracuse. A little later the society worshipped

Dunwick, Photo.   THE METHODIST EPISCOPAL CHURCH AND PARSONAGE.

Burns E. Parkhurst, was born in the town of Mexico in this county and in 1862, August 21, enlisted from that town in the 147th Regiment New York Vol. Inft. He was promoted to corporal and served during the civil war until June 29, 1865, when he was discharged at Washington, D. C. In the Chancellorsville campaign the 147th Regiment was attached to the Second Brigade, First Division, First Corps Army of the Potomac which was directed to cross the Rappahannock River below Fredericksburg at a place called Fitzhugh Crossing or Pollocks Mill Creek. The 147th was the first regiment to cross the pontoon bridge to the south bank of the river. In the afternoon of April 30, 1863, Corporal Parkhurst was assigned to an exposed position of great peril which is best told in his own words as follows: We were ordered to throw up breastworks, and as soon as we commenced to do so, the enemy began to fire at us from a battery in front with 12 pound shells. Our batteries in our rear replied to the enemy, firing over our heads. One of their guns fired to the left of our regiment and one to the right, the middle gun firing directly at us. The regiment was commanded by Col. John G. Butler and Company F, to which I belonged, was commanded by Capt. H. G. Lee. Soon after the firing began I was given an order by Capt. Lee to occupy position in front of this center gun of the enemy and when it was fired to give the order: 'Down!' when the men by falling flat upon the ground were enabled to protect themselves until the shell had passed over. I occupied this position, exposed to the enemy's fire from this gun, for over an hour, until the breastworks were high enough to protect the men and it was no longer necessary for me to remain, when by order I resumed my place in the company. As I stood looking into the mouth of the gun the flame which sprung forth at every discharge seemed to almost scorch my face. I was a mere boy and the exper-

B. E. PARKHURST. J. FRANCIS PARKHURST.
JOHN W. PARKHURST. WARD B. PARKHURST.

in the village school house, until the court house was built in 1819, where service was held for a few years. This appointment was then a part of the old Sandy Creek circuit, and so remained until 1831, when Pulaski first appeared as a separate circuit or station. During this period the charge was served by some of the strong men of the conference, among whom were such well known fathers in ministry as Issac Puffer, Elias Bowen, George Gary, Enoch Barnes, Elisha Wheeler, and Schuyler Hoes. In 1832 William Ward Ninde the father of the late Bishop Ninde was the pastor, and the society erected a good church building on the site now occupied by Charles B. Hibbard on Salina street. The presiding elder, Josiah Keyes was present at the dedication of the church; and the pastor, Mr. Ninde, preached what was regarded as a great sermon. In 1834 the Sunday school was first organized, meeting in the gallery at the close of the morning service.

(Concluded on page 53.)

N. PHILBRICK'S RESIDENCE.

H. IRVING PRATT,
School Commissioner Third District.

ience was a terrible shock to my system, especially as my attention was soon after I had taken my position called to the fact that when I stood erect my head was in line with the course of the shells. I received a report of this service from Col. Butler in the fall of 1897 over 34 years after the battle of Pollocks Mill Creek, Va.; but it is now on record in the War Department at Washington, D. C., with honorable mention by Col. Butler for gallant and meritorious conduct." Mr. Parkhurst has a medal from the state of New York as a Gettysburg veteran awarded in July 1893, thirty years after the battle of Gettysburg which was fought July 1st, 2nd and 3rd, 1863. Soon after the close of the civil war Mr. Parkhurst came into this town and for over twenty-five years has resided in Pulaski as a lawyer and for over twenty years has been a justice of the peace. In connection with his son John W. Parkhurst he has carried on a large insurance business which for a number of years past has been conducted principally by John W. Parkhurst. With another son Ward B. Parkhurst they carry on the No-Fly Works, located at Pulaski, N. Y., for the manufacture of No-Fly originated by Ward B. Parkhurst which is used for the relief of cattle, horses, and other animals from all insects. Burns E. Parkhurst is a great-grandson of Colonel Johnathan Parkhurst who participated in the battle of Oswego in the war of 1812.

Harvey Irving Pratt.—Many of the sterling young men of cities and towns in various parts of the country look back to the town of Orwell as their birthplace and it is with pleasure they recall the names of people who have been recorded among the sons of that town. On June 1, 1877, to Mr. and Mrs. Ralph Pratt was born a son, and in the years which have since elapsed that son has grown to manhood and to-day he is best known to this county and a good portion of the state as Commissioner Harvey Irving Pratt, commissioner

of the schools of the Third Commissioner District of Oswego county. His educational training includes a course in the Orwell Grammar school, a course in the Pulaski High school, graduation from Rochester Business University and a course in the Oswego Normal school. He has had two years' experience as teacher in public schools and was appointed school commissioner in March, 1901, and as this work goes to press is the nominee of the republican party to succeed himself in this fall election. Mr. Pratt is secretary of the State School Commissioners' Association, and secretary of the Oswego County Christian Endeavor Union.

Oron V. Davis, the jeweler, located in Pulaski in 1877, immediately after having served a regular apprenticeship of seven years with Becker & Lathrop, Syracuse, N. Y., where he received the advantage of a thorough technical and mechanical training. Mr. Davis commenced business in a modest way by renting a show window in a clothing store, two doors south of his present location. The business prospered and soon a show-case and counter were added. More commodious quarters were secured Jan. 1, 1881, in the grocery store of Mr. R. L. Parsons, who was closing out his stock to retire from trade, April 1, 1881, the entire store was leased, refitted, new show-cases added and the stock enlarged. The building having been burned in the great conflagration of Oct. 6, 1881, the stock was then removed to the residence then occupied by Mr. Davis on the west side of Broad street opposite the south park. That winter Mr. Davis purchased the store lot formerly

Dunwick, Photo.
O. V. DAVIS' JEWELRY STORE.

CAROLINE E. CLARKE (Mrs. R. L. Ingersoll.)
ROBERT L. INGERSOLL.

wale, cut glass, watches and jewelry, the north side. Special attention is given to watch repairing, artistic hand engraving and optical work. Mr. Edward L. Davis, eldest son of the proprietor, is employed in the store.

Robert Leroy Ingersoll, banker, capitalist, and manufacturer, was identified with the momentary interests of Pulaski from 1847 until his death. He was born in New Berlin, N. Y., June 5, 1819, son of Ebenezer Ingersoll and Sarah Rich, being a descendent of John Ingersoll, of Salem, Mass., 1629, dating back to the Saxons, and of Thomas Rich, of Springfield, Mass., 1630, of English blood royal to the Normans. His father was a farmer and he was the eldest of a large family. In 1830 his family came to Oswego county and settled in Sandy Creek. He attended the district schools and Mexico Academy. Then he learned the wagon trade and worked with his father and then for himself until 1847. That year he came to Pulaski, bought what is now known as the Froude block, in which he had his office, and engaged in the manufacture of carriages, employing a large number of men. The factory was on Mill street, on the lands occupied by E. D. Forman's livery barn and where S. C. Huntington's law office recently stood. For years this business was a leading industry of the village.

In 1857 he took in as a partner, Mr. Thomas Ingersoll, (who learned his trade in these shops) under the style of Ingersoll & Co. In 1860 he sold his interest to Mr. J. R. Greenwood. In

occupied by him and in the spring erected the building here illustrated. It was ready for occupancy in July, 1882, and is a model of convenience, having been designed to meet the special requirements of the business. The stock consists of such goods as are usually found in a first-class jewelry store. The clock and optical department occupy the south side of the store and the silver-

VIEWS OF THE ROBERT L. INGERSOLL PROPERTY.

1866 he purchased Mr. Greenwood's interest, also the Larrabee factory, and the firm under the name of T. R. Ingersoll & Co., R. L. being the Co., began business on Jefferson street. In 1867 Mr. L. J. Hawley became a partner. In 1871 Mr. Ingersoll retired from the firm.

In 1867 he, with others, purchased the planing mill and sash and blind factory of David Bennett, on the north side of Salmon river below Jefferson street bridge and engaged in contracting and building. He became sole owner of this business in 1876 and continued it until his death.

He owned a large amount of real estate, village and farm property. In 1854 Mr. Ingersoll established the first bank in Pulaski called the Pulaski Bank. Associated in its organization were a number of well known citizens. Mr. Ingersoll was the largest stock holder and Mr. Thomas W.

with its patrons merited the confidence and commendation it received from the merchants, manufacturers and farmers during its existence until 1886. It occupied the quarters of the Pulaski Bank.

Mr. Ingersoll was a Jeffersonian democrat, yet such was his popularity that when he ran for president of the village in a strong republican town he not only was elected but the entire democratic ticket. During his term Jefferson street, then a crooked one, was straightened, making it one of the prettiest of the village. He also served as supervisor and was a member of Pulaski Lodge, F. & A. M.

He married, Nov, 16, 1842, Miss Caroline E. Clarke, of Lorraine, N. Y., daughter of James H. Clarke and Lydia L. Atwood, a descendant of Joseph Clarke, Newport, R. I., 1638, and Dr. Thomas

VIEWS OF THE PROPERTY OF MRS. N. M. RICH.
The North End.   The South End.

Dixson the next largest. The bank was operated under a state charter and its authorized capital was $100,000. Although Mr. Ingersoll was the youngest director he was elected president and served until 1857 when he assumed the duties of cashier and continued in that office until the retirement of the bank's charter in 1862. The bank did a prosperous business and stood on the site now occupied by the Pulaski House.

In 1862 the private bank of R. L. Ingersoll & Co. was formed, Mr. Thomas W. Dixson being a co-partner. Mr. Ingersoll gave personal attention to the bank and Mr. W. B. Dixson, son of Thomas W. Dixson, became its cashier. The R. L. Ingersoll & Co.'s bank occupied a conspicuous place in the business of the village. Its career was full of honor and the liberal policy it pursued

Atwood, Hartford, Conn., 1660, each dating back several centuries of English gentry. They had six children: Charles Leroy, who died in childhood; George D., who still lives in the village, owns a large block and is engaged in business; Robert F. B. died in 1885; Frank D., living in Chicago has two sons, the only living Ingersoll line of descent; Miss Maud M., in New York City; Anna A. in Syracuse, whose first husband was Frank H. Dimock, of Quincy, Ill., by whom she had two children, Maud I. and Robert Ingersoll. Her second husband was Nellis Marathon Rich, formerly of Altmar, N. Y. Mrs. Rich is treasurer of Onondaga Chapter, Daughters of the American Revolution; president of Hiawatha Society, Children of the American Revolution; a graduate of St. Mary's, Burlington, N. J; a lineal descendent

Dunwick, Photo.   L. J. MACY.

of seven Revolutionary patriots, a Colonial governor and several persons prominent in the civil and military life of Colonial times. She is also prominent in the social and club life of the city. Mr. Rich is connected with a wholesale dry goods house.

Mrs. Ingersoll, resides with her daughter, Mrs. Rich. Mr. Ingersoll was one of Pulaski's most public spirited citizens and he and Mrs. Ingersoll were very prominent in its social life. The Ingersoll property has been in the family since 1866. Mr. Ingersoll died Aug. 2?, 1886. Mrs. Ingersoll sold the residence in 1897. The remainder of the Ingersoll Pulaski property is still owned by Mrs. Rich.

L. J. Macy is quite prominently identified with the order of masonry and other fraternities in Pulaski and vicinity and has taken a conspicuous hand in the politics of the town. He has been engaged in the hardware and plumbing business in Pulaski since 1882 at which time he bought the shop and store of Lyman & Beadle—a business which he now carries on in a large and liberal way. In 1869 he entered the employ of that firm and remained with them until he succeeded to their business, acquiring a practical knowledge in all of its branches. Mr. Macy served four years as supervisor of the town of Richland and was an active legislator for his constituency.

Mr. Macy was born in Chatham Four Corners, town of Ghent, Columbia county, N. Y., in 1848, of English parentage, his father and mother both being Quakers whose ancestors left England in 1632 and settled in Nantucket. His parents moved to Oswego county in 1855 and settled on a farm in the town of Sandy Creek. In 1861 they moved to Pulaski, where Mr. Macy has since resided. He was educated in the district schools and the Pulaski academy. By industry and frugality he earned the capital with which to start in business for himself. In 1869 he joined the Pulaski Fire Department and served faithfully until 1885, holding the positions of captain and chief engineer. He was also two years in the village board of trustees. He joined the Pulaski lodge of Free and Accepted Masons, No. 415, in April 1871, and was its master in 1879 and '80. In the former year he was exalted in Mexico Chapter No. 135, R. A. M. and in 1885 he assisted in organizing Pulaski Chapter No. 279, F. & A. M., serving two years as Most Excellent High Priest. In 1880 he assisted in organizing Pulaski Lodge A. O. U. W. and was its first Master. He is a member of Lake Ontario Commandery, Knights of Templars of Oswego and has been for years a director for the Masonic Life Association of Oswego county. He is one of the charter members of Pulaski Lodge I. O. O. F.

In January, 1885, he married Cora B. Austin of Pulaski, to whom one child was born, Cora Flossie.

Mr. Macy was mustered into the order of Sons of Veterans as a charter member of A. S. Warner Camp, No. 105, and was elected its first captain. In 1891 he was appointed Aide de Camp on Commander C. H. Holmes' staff and in June, 1892, at Amsterdam, was elected Junior Vice Division Commander of New York State. In June, 1893, he was elected Senior Vice Division Commander and in June, 1894, at Middleport was unanimously elected Division Commander at Syracuse, the

A. S. WARNER CAMP, NO. 105, SONS OF VETERANS.
1, W. J. Leonard, Captain; 2, R. C. Pirnie, 1st Lieutenant; 3, W. F. Corcoran, 2nd Lieutenant; 4, B. G. Seamans, Camp Council; 5, J. W. Parkhurst, Sergeant of Guard; 6, W. T. Morton, Picket Guard; 7, N. G. Ehle, Chaplain; 8, Henry Hinman, First Sergeant; 9, L. J. Macy, Quartermaster Sergeant; 10, Frank Prouty, Color Sergeant; 11, Frank Hollis, Camp Guard; 12, C. R. North, and 13, C. B. Burch, Past Captains.

W. D. STREETER, SUPERVISOR.

next year, he was re-elected to that post, the first to be honored with a second term. He is a member of the Order of Elks, Oswego lodge, and has been for several years.

The Monday Historical Club was organized in November, 1900, with twenty-five members, but during the next year the number was limited to twenty. No one is received under twenty years of age and no school girl is eligible. Its object is the study of history and it has been so far occupied with English history and the historical plays of Shakespeare. Meetings are held each Monday afternoon, excepting during the summer months. The hour of meeting has been from three to five o'clock. On the last Monday of each month a committee of four members serve a five o'clock tea. Once each year a banquet is held when the members are privileged to each invite one guest. The officers are: Mrs. Francis B Betts, President; Mrs. Sadie M. Tollner, Vice-President; Miss Mary L. Paul, Secretary; Mrs. Henry B. Clark, Treasurer; Mrs. Nathan B. Smith, Leader; Mrs. Charles E. Low, Assistant Leader.

Col. A. S. Warner Camp, No. 105, Sons of Veterans, Division of New York, U. S. A., was mustered in October 24, 1890, by Capt. M. S. Furgeson of Sandy Creek, with sixteen charter members. The following were elected its first officers: Lewis J. Macy, Captain; Calvin B. Burch, First Lieutenant; Warren W. Warner, Second Lieutenant; Newton G. Ehle, Chaplain; John W. Parkhurst, First Sergeant; Geo. M. Box, Quartermaster Sergeant; Henry W. Hinman, Color Sergeant; Gerrit S. Warner, Sergeant of Guard; Clinton J. Bean, Corporal of Guard; Grant Calkins, Camp Guard; John Burr, Picket Guard; Chas. Filkins, Principal Musician; G. S. Warner, Chas. Paddock and W. C. Warner, Camp Counsel. From the day of its muster its growth has been rapid, and it has found a place in the front

rank of the order and has been honored with Division Commander, Senior Vice-Division Commander, two Junior Vice-Division Commanders, two Division Adjutants, Division Quartermaster, Assistant Inspector General and twelve Past Captains. Since its organization it has mustered 103 members. Its present officers are: W. J. Leonard, Captain; R. C. Pirnie, First Lieutenant; W. F. Corcoran, Second Lieutenant; Newton G. Ehle, Chaplain; Henry Hinman, First Sergeant; L. J. Macy, Quartermaster Sergeant; J. W. Parkhurst, Sergeant of Guard; P. A. Filkins, Corporal of Guard; Frank Prouty, Color Sergeant; Frank Hollis, Camp Guard; W. T. Morton, Picket Guard; B. G. Seamans, Principal Musician.

W. D. Streeter, the supervisor for the town of Richland, first elected to that position in 1899 and re-elected in 1901, has been prominent for several years in the republican politics of the town and county. Conducting a large store in Richland village, in a building which he erected near the railroad station and opened for trade in 1893, he has long been engaged in a general mercantile business. He is also the postmaster of Richland appointed to that position in July following McKinley's first election (July 1897) and continued therein for the second term. As a member of the board of supervisors Mr. Streeter takes an active part in the proceedings of that body, watching legislation with zealous care in the interests of his constituents.

Mr. Streeter was born in the town of Richland, November 15, 1856. When he was a young man his parents moved to Ellisburg, Jefferson county, where he divided his time working on a farm and in a store and teaching school. Locating at

R. W. BOX, POSTMASTER.

ST. JOHN'S CHURCH, PULASKI, N. Y.

Orwell in 1884, he resumed farming for three years and then bought out the store of F. B. Woodbury. Three years later he moved to Richland and succeeded the firm of L. C. Bullock & Co. in the lower end of the village. His store and stock of goods were destroyed by fire Aug. 5, 1893. Three days later, Aug. 8, he had a new stock of goods in a new place ready for business, getting back into trade in a remarkably brief space of time. This was only temporary, as he at once began the erection of his new block, where he had his goods ready for customers in the surprisingly short time of about two months. In the meantime, March 5, 1902, he bought out the stock of G. H. Mellen and for a time ran two stores. Mr. Streeter and Libbie M., the daughter of Ira Cummings of Boylston, were married Jan. 21, 1878. Their only child is Mabel E., the wife of Lyman E. Jewell.

Mr. Streeter is one of the Elks of Oswego, a charter member of Spring Brook Lodge, I. O. O F., of Richland, of which he was the first noble grand, and a member of the Pulaski encampment.

St. John the Evangelist's church was erected in 1888, under the direction of Rev. J. M. Varrily. With the generous help of the Catholics at that time and of his many non-Catholic friends, Father Varrily succeeded in his enterprise and built the pretty little church of St. John which stands to-day as an ornament to the village of Pulaski. In July, 1888, the corner stone of the new church was laid by the rural Dean, the Very Rev. M. J. Barry, of Oswego, who preached the sermon for the occasion, a large gathering of people being present and $300 being collected. On Jan. 16, 1889, the dedication took place, the Rt. Rev. P. A. Ludden, Bishop of the Diocese, officiating. The Very Rev. M. J. Barry, celebrated the first Mass in the new church and Rev. S. A. Preisser, of Syracuse, preached the dedicatory sermon. On June 11, 1889, Rev. Father Varrily was called to Massena Springs to act as pastor and there he remained until he was called again to Winchendon, Mass., where he is to-day, faithfully exercising

ST. ANN'S CHURCH, COLOSSE, N. Y.

his sacred functions of a Priest, with the Rev. John Conway of the Church of the Immaculate Heart of Mary, in the Diocese of Springfield. Father Varrily was succeeded by the late Rev. Chas. Durocher, who was a good old man, loved and respected by all classes of people. His death occurred on the 11th of April, 1899. During the following fourteen months St. John's church was in charge of Rev. John Lindsman, of Oswego, and on Dec. 20, 1899, the present young pastor took full charge. Ever since his appointment as pastor Rev. Theodore Provost's labors in Pulaski have

REV. THEODORE PROVOST.

REV. THEODORE PROVOST'S RESIDENCE, PULASKI

Huested, Photo.
BOX'S DEPARTMENT STORE.

active workers. The present officers are Mrs. F. P. Betts, President; Miss Anna Lacy, Vice-President; Miss Marguerita Hinman, Secretary; Miss Emily L. Clark, Treasurer; J. T. Wright, Corresponding Secretary; Miss Lizzie Fuller, Junior Work.

The First Methodist Episcopal Church.—
[Concluded—see pages 45 and 46.]

In July 1840 the old Black River conference met in this church, the presiding elder being the venerable Bishop Roberts and the Sunday service was held in a grove on the river bank. The present commodious church edifice was built in 1860 during the pastorate of Rev. Lemuel Clark, at a cost of several thousand dollars; and it was thoroughly remodeled and improved in 1888 during the first year of Rev. Alexander Bramley's pastorate. A second session of the annual conference was held in 1861, Bishop Baker presiding. It was about the time of the fall of Fort Sumter, and the American people were under intense excitment. Dr. Hiram Mattison one of the strongest anti slavery men in the country delivered a great speech, and Rev. Nathan Salisbury offered a prayer, probably never excelled in fervency, pathos and power, by any that was ever offered in this church. Among the many interesting items connected with the history of this church it is related that one C. C. West was appointed by the pastor in 1831 to lead the Sunday evening prayer meeting, the pastor preaching elsewhere. He held this position until he moved to the west in 1852. And for many years he furnished the lights and fuel for the church services. The records of church membership before 1840 have been lost. The most extensive revival the charge has ever known occurred in 1857 under the labors of Rev. Samuel B. Crosier when one hundred and sixty were received.

The Rev. Sidney O. Barnes, A. M., the pastor of the First Methodist Episcopal church of Pulaski, N. Y., was born in Joliett, Illinois. He prepared for college in Red Creek Union Academy, Wayne County, of this state, where he also taught for two years. Entering Genesee College, since incorporated in Syracuse University, in the

been very successful both spiritually and financially. The congregation counts a few more members and its finances have largely increased. Many repairs on the church have been made. The better part of Father Provost's work is the building of his new and beautiful little church at Altmar which was dedicated the past summer. Father Provost has also bought and furnished a house of his own near the church in Pulaski where his young niece, Miss Antoinette Provost presides.

The Young People's Society of Christian Endeavor connected with the Congregational church was organized in 1888 and has proved a useful adjunct. For over three years the prayer meetings of the society have been held on Monday evenings from 7:15 to 8:00 p. m., the large attendance of young people proving the wisdom of this departure. The society is a regular contributor to the support of the church at home and abroad. There are about twenty-five enrolled as

Huested, Photo.   JOHN N. DALY'S CLOTHING STORE.

GEORGE W. FULLER.
The Oldest Merchant in Business in Pulaski.

Sophomore class in 1859, he graduated in 1862 receiving second honors; and in 1865 he was advanced to the masters degree. After his graduation he served one year as principal of the academy where he had prepared for college. On July 1st, 1863 he was married to Miss Anna Hamilton of Conquest, N. Y., one of his school mates, and for nine months he served a charge under the elder. In the spring of 1864 he was admitted on trial in the Black River conference, now the Nothern New York conference, of which he has ever since been a member. In 1873 he was chosen secretary of the conference and served for eight years in that capacity, until appointed presiding elder of the St. Lawrence district in 1880. After filling out the term of four years on this district he returned to the pastorate, being stationed at Ilion for the ensuing three years. In 1895 he was appointed presiding elder of the Watertown district, residing in Watertown until the end of the term in April 1901, when he was appointed to Pulaski. Among his pastoral appointments have been Boonville, Clayton,

Adams, Lowville, Potsdam and Herkimer. He was elected by his brethren one of the delegates to represent them in the general conference of 1880, and also in 1884. He has been blessed with two children a son and daughter, both of whom reside in Watertown, where they are in business.

G. W. Fuller, the oldest merchant doing business in Pulaski, to-day, came to this village from Cazenovia, in 1840, with Dr. Newell Wright to clerk in his store. Dr. Wright, whose place of business was on the site of Meacham's drug store, finally failed, and in 1843 Mr. Fuller began the dry goods business on his own account. Five years later he sold out and went into the old red mill with one named Porter, from which he retired four years later and went into the hardware, stove and tinware business with Mr. Norton. In 1855 the firm sold out to Daniel B. Meacham and on Jan. 1, 1857, Mr. Fuller began the drug trade on the site where he is still in business with his son, Mr. George H. Fuller. In the big fire of 1881 he burned out and soon after he had erected the large, handsome building which he has since occupied. Mr. Fuller was born in Cazenovia, March 11, 1818. For one of his years, 84, he is yet quite active mentally and physically.

Rev. Jesse Burdett Felt was born at Arlington, Vt., and received his education in the schools of his native state. On leaving college he entered the work of the Young Men's Christian Association, with which he was identified for over ten years, first as an Assistant Secretary in the New York city association, then as General Secretary, being located successively at Ogdensburg and Clifton Springs, N. Y., Springfield, Mass., Hot Springs, Ark., and Warsaw, N. Y. While organizing an association in the latter place he was called to the pastorate of the Congregational church at Gainesville, a

Huested, Photo.   FULLER'S DRUG STORE.

MRS. W. H. HILL.   W. H. HILL.

William H. Hill was for several years an associate in charge of Pierrepont estates in Oswego and Jefferson counties and had his headquarters in the old land office in this village. Mrs. Hill (Miss Evelyn) is the daughter of the late William Constable Pierrepont of Pierrepont Manor and it was at her father's request that her husband brought his family from the west where they were then living, and took control of the large Pierrepont land interest. It was in 1862 that Mr. and Mrs. Hill took up their residence here, and made it their permanent home, first living in a house on the park and subsequently becoming domiciled in their prettily situated home on Salina street. Both were constant attendants at the Episcopal church in which denomination Mrs. Hill was brought up at home.

Mr. Hill was born at Western, Oneida county, Jan. 14, 1816. His father and mother were Quaker preachers and he did not have the advantage of a liberal education. He first went into business with his brother in Rome, N. Y.; during his sojourn there he was married to Miss Evelyn Pierrepont Feb. 19, 1861. The business at Rome not proving successful he moved to the west, but his services being required by his father-in-law here, he soon after came to Pulaski.

The Pierreponts as is generally known were one of the oldest and most aristocratic of the Northern New York families who were numbered among the lauded proprietors of this state early in the last century. Hezekiah Pierrepont, Mrs. Hill's grandfather, was lord of the manor, his estates consisting of several thousands of acres in Frauklin, Oswego, Jefferson and St. Lawrence counties and the old Manor House which is still standing at Pierrepont Manor, the village to which it gave its name, is the place where she was born.

Mr. and Mrs. Hill have two children, William P., who was born in Pulaski Nov. 3, 1866, and is

neighboring village. Being licensed to preach by the Genesee Association of Congregational churches he began work in this field July 5, 1891, In connection with his work at Gainesville he preached at Rock Glen, a near-by hamlet, where under his leadership a church was soon organized and a church building erected. On Nov. 1, 1892, he was ordained by a council composed of ministers and delegates from the leading Congregational churches of Western New York, Rev. F. S. Fitch, D.D., of Buffalo, being moderator. In the spring of '93 he accepted a call from the Congregational church at Carthage, where he remained for five and a half years. During this period the church which for many years had received aid from the Home Missionary Society became self-supporting. Its edifice was enlarged and remodeled, and its membership more than doubled. In October, 1898, Mr. Felt received and accepted a unanimous call to the pastorate of the Pulaski church, and Dec. 18th began his work in this place. In September, 1883, he was united in marriage to Miss Bertha Boardman, of Clifton Springs, N. Y. They have one child, Dorothy, born at Warsaw, N. Y., Feb. 22, 1891.

The Salmon River House was thus named by J. A. Ford in May, 1849, who at that time became the owner of the property, purchasing what was previously known as Brainard's Hotel.

Huested, Photo.   MRS. W. H. HILL'S RESIDENCE.

Dunwick, Photo.   T. S. MEACHAM'S RESIDENCE.

now in Canada, and Mary Pierrepont Hill, born here Oct. 7, 1862, who is the wife of John B. Etheridge. They are living at Salem, Mass., and have two children living, Sarah Harrington, and William Hill Etheridge. John Pierrepont Etheridge their oldest son is dead.

Great Fire of 1881.—At four o'clock in the morning of October 6, 1881, which was Thursday, a destructive fire broke out in the bakery in the rear of M. L. Hollis's store and before it could be put out it swept, according to the local paper, that portion of the town "from North Park to South Park on the west side of Jefferson street and from the Froude block to the iron bridge over Salmon river." In three hours time the main part of the ruined district was wrapped in flames. Oswego being called upon for help, sent a company with an engine which did good service, taking water from the raceway below the factory. This structure and the Froude block narrowly escaped taking fire. The losses footed up between $200,000 and $250,000. The next day a scene of ruin and desolation which Pulaski never before or since experienced, was presented to the eye. The parks were strewn with all manner of portable objects, laying as they were dropped when hurriedly dragged from the burning buildings. Those named as losers were:—Dr. J. N. Betts; H. B. Clark; W. H. Gray, the Salmon River House; M. Levy, clothing; George W. Douglas; Pulaski National Bank; R. L. Ingersoll & Co., Bank; M. L. Hollis, crockery; G. W. Fuller & Son, drugs;

C. C. Wood, dry goods, R. L. Parsons, clothing; R. S. Avery, photographer; Box & Corey, drugs; Mrs. L. E. & E. J. Box, milliners; Ed. Forman, livery; Joseph David, wagonmaker; J. M. Sampson, painter; G. D. Ingersoll, meat market; C. D. Clark; N. B. Smith, law; Mrs. E. D. Forman, milliner; B. D. Salisbury, building; W. F. Austin, building; D. A. King, law; Ringgold Fire Company; L. R. Muzzy, Pulaski Democrat; A. N. Beadle, hardware; H. H. Lyman, building; C. B. Hibbard, jewelery; Dr. H. W. Caldwell; R. Box, furniture; B. E. Parkhurst, law; C. A. Gurley, building; Dr. N. A. Caldwell; G. A. Bayne, photographer; D. B. Meacham & Son, drugs; J. Dillenbeck, building; Dr. F. J. Bradner; Adelbert Meacham, law; the Postoffice; Dr. E. F. Kelley; Wm. Bliss, restaurant; Capt. L. M. Tyler, livery; George B. Washington, grocery; Lucius Jones, dry goods; Wm. June, two buildings; O. V. Davis, jewelry; John F. Box, drugs; Miss Alice Tifft, millinery; A. F. Betts, merchant tailor; T. J. Bumpus, grocer; C. R. Jones, dry goods; A. S. Warner, building; E. H. Minot, insurance.

"What I Can,"—A society of young ladies of the First Baptist church, has been recently organized to be known as the "What I Can Society," with the motto "She hath done what she could." It meets each month and is one of the most promising societies connected with the church. The officers of this new missionary society are: President, Miss Laura B. Wilson; vice president, Miss Jessie McRobie; secretary, Miss Clara Gurley; treasurer, Miss Grace Washington.

RESIDENCE OF SPECIALIST F. H. CROSS AND HIS SON, WILLARD G. CROSS.

From old Kodak Photo.   MRS. M. A. RHODES' RESIDENCE.

Pulaski in the Rebellion.—The town contributed 277 men to the union armies and navy in the war of 1861–'5, several of whom attained commissioned offices. The first news of the surrender of Fort Sumter, published in the Pulaski Democrat, April 18, 1861, was immediately followed by the raising of the flag to the top of several buildings in the village. On April 26 and 27 union meetings were held to set on foot a military company. Tucker hall resounded with patriotic eloquence, and $1,100 was subscribed to be used for the support of the families of those who should volunteer their services. Other meetings in Pulaski followed, on April 2 and May 2 and 4. Fifty names were enrolled, and on Saturday, May 11, the company was sworn in with the following officers: Captain, E. W. Peckham; First Lieutenant, S. A. McCarty; Ensign, Wm. H. Smith; First Sergeant, S. D. Seamans; Second Sergeant, George P. Rich; Third Sergeant, W. O. Moffitt; Fourth Sergeant, James A. Bentley; First Corporal, F. M. Niles; Second Corporal, George Knowles; Third Corporal, G. E. Wood; Fourth Corporal, F. Baker. On May 15 a torchlight procession paraded the streets, and on May 16 the volunteers, between 50 and 60, departed for Albany. On the Monday following, 30 more followed them, such was the patriotism and order in the cause of the union

displayed by the citizens of the town of Richland and the village of Pulaski. Upon reaching the capital the men were quartered at the Adams House until they were attached to the Thirteenth regiment and ordered to Elmira. The authorities rejected Captain Peckham, and so dissatisfied were the men he had led out of Pulaski that the company was broken up and the men were scattered among different companies and regiments. Some of them were attached to the Thirty-seventh regiment, the Irish rifles, and others remained with the Thirteenth. The former were incorporated in a Cattaraugus company, Captain Clark, and the latter in Co. I, Capt. George B. Rich. Five enlisted at the Brooklyn navy yard and were attached to the steamer North Carolina. They were Calvin L. Conant, George and Thomas Morton, James M. Williams and Reuben Nobles.

The First Town Officers in Richland were chosen at a meeting held in the spring of 1807 at the residence of Ephraim Brewster, east of the village of Pulaski. They were, supervisor, Joseph Hurd; town clerk, William Hale; assessors, Geo. Harding, John Meacham and Joseph Chase; overseers of the poor, Isaac Meacham and Gershom Hale; highway commissioners, Simon Meacham, Elias Howe and Jonathan Rhodes; collector for

Dunwick, Photo.   C. C. CLARK'S RESIDENCE.

Dunwick, Photo.   FRANK McCHESNEY'S RESIDENCE.

the towns of Sandy Creek, Orwell, Boylston and the north part of the town of Richland, Elias Howe; collector for Albion and south part of Richland, Pliny Jones; constables, Elias Howe, Justus St. John and Pliny Jones; fence viewers, Asahel Hurd, Joseph Chase and Gershom Hale; pound-master, George Harding; pathmasters, Nathan W. Noyes, Wm. Robinson, Timothy Balch, Elias Howe, Gershom Hale, Ephraim Brewster, Jonathan Rhodes, Timothy Kellogg and Isaac Leigh.

The Woman's Missionary Society of the Congregational church was organized in March, 1877, about a year after the organization of the New York State Branch of the Woman's Board of Missions, and was one of the first to become auxiliary to that body. The only officer elected the first year was a treasurer, Miss Hulda L. Lane, but ten collectors were appointed, and at the close of the year $20 was sent to the state treasury. The following year at a meeting addressed by Mrs. Tracy, of Marsovan, Turkey, a more complete organization was effected, and the following officers were elected: President, Mrs. Jas. Douglas; secretary, Mrs. Samuel Riker; treasurer, Mrs. Robert Gillespie. At a subsequent meeting the society decided to assume a share in the support of Mrs. Tracy. During these early years the money raised was all devoted to the work of foreign missions, but in 1885 the society became auxiliary to the Home Missionary Union, and for many years was a distinctively Home Mission-

ary organization. In February, 1899, the society was re-organized on a more comprehensive basis, and a systematic study of Christiam missions, both home and foreign, has been undertaken. The work of the six national missionary societies of the Congregational denomination, not omitting the special field of the Woman's Board, is taken in turn. The meetings are held monthly at the homes of its members with an annual tea-meeting to which the gentlemen and young people are invited. At present the officers are: President, Mrs. Jesse B. Felt; vice presidents, Mrs. H. B. Clark and Mrs. G. H. Fuller; secretary, Miss Anna B. Gurley; treasurer, Mrs. Ella M. Wright.

Early Schools. —The first school in the town of Richland was taught by Milly Ellis in the summer of 1808. The first school in Pulaski village was taught in a building erected by Jeremiah A. Matthewson for a blacksmith shop, near the south end of the hotel which he conducted for some time. The teacher, Rebecca Cross was succeeded by Mrs. James Harmon, who was succeeded by Miss A. Hinman. The next school in the village was conducted by Pliny Jones in a log building owned by Mr. Matthewson. The first school building was built on the premises afterward owned by W. H. Hill, but two months after being completed it was burned. School was then held in a building owned by Mr. Bush, which stood on the site of the subsequent residence of George W. Wood. Pliny Jones, however, soon opened his house for school purposes and the

Dunwick, Photo.   GEORGE H. BEEMAN'S RESIDENCE.

Huested, Photo.   ROBERT D. GILLESPIE'S RESIDENCE.

The Ladies' Guild of St. James's church was organized in 1886 for the purpose of aiding the church in a general way. The officers elected were Mrs. Sophia Cross, president; Miss Fannie Stevens, vice president, and Mrs. Cora Betts, secretary and treasurer. The present officers are Miss Louise Foreman, president; Mrs. Sophia Cross, vice president; Mrs. M. P. Parsons, treasurer, and Mrs. Helen Hutchins, secretary.

The Ladies' Aid Society, Congregational church, has been organized for many years. The society raises about $100 each year to assist in paying the expenses of the church. The present officers are: Mrs. Ella K. Wright, president; Miss Anna B. Gurley, secretary and treasurer.

next year a school house was erected on the site afterwards occupied by Cross's land office. Later it was moved to the subsequent site of the old Baptist church. The next school house was a brick structure built on the site of the Congregational church, and after it was demolished school was held in the church edifice. Select schools have flourished at different periods, notably those of M. W Southworth in Masonic hall in 1821, and of A. Bond in 1848.

Pulaski in 1835.—The "168th regiment, 38th brigade infantry, militia of the state of New York," had its headquarters in Pulaski in 1835. Nathan Stoddard was the colonel commanding and Alvin Strong and Harry Brooks, of this village were captains. In a copy of the Pulaski Banner, dated Sept. 9, 1835, there appear two "runaway notices" in which John P. Leavitt, of Albion, and Johnathan Ferguson, of Richland, advertise for their mis-ing apprentices. The village trustees offer a reward of $250 for the apprehension of the perpetrators of "sundry acts of outrage" by which the peace was disturbed. Those who advertised in the paper and were naturally the only husiness places of consequence in the village at that time were Baker & Allen, cash store; Joseph Porthouse, blacksmith; T. C. Baker, general store; Newell Wright, general store; Stevens, French & Pearce, oil mill; John L. Molther, general store; J. D. & F. Lane and John H. Wells, general stores; E. S. Salisbury, tailor; G. Dean, barber; John Box, jr., blacksmith.

Supervisors of the town of Richland from the beginning to the present time are as follows: Joseph Hurd, 1807-'8; John C. Pride, 1809-'16, '20-'1, '23, '25-'6; Simon Meacham, 1817-'19, '22, '24; Thomas C. Baker, 1827; Robert Gillespie, 1828-'9, '31-'3, '37-'8; Isaac Stearns, 1830, '34, '36; L. D. Mansfield, 1835; M. W. Matthews, 1839-'41; Bradley Higgins, 1842-'3; Dr. H. F. Noyes, 1844, '52; A. Crandall, 1845-'6; Casper C. West, 1847; E. M. Hill, 1848-'51; N. W. Wardwell, 1853; S. H. Meacham, 1854; James A. Clark, 1855-'6, '59-'60; John T. McCarty, '1857-'8; Isaac Fellows, 1861-'2; Sewell T. Gates, 1863-'5; William H. Gray, 1866; G. T. Peckham, 1867-'9; Dr. James N. Betts, 1870, '80; Henry H. Lyman, 1871-'2; William B. Dixon, 1873-'8; Robert L. Ingersoll, 1879; Lawson R. Muzzy, 1881-'2, '86-7; Thomas R. Ingersoll,

Dunwick, Photo.   J. J. DILLENBECK'S RESIDENCE.

B. D. RANDALL.

1883; Richard W. Box, 1884–'5, '92–'3; Isaac J. Rich, 1888–'91, '94–'5; L. J. Macy, 1896–'8; W. D. Streetor, 1899–1902.

B. D. Randall, the well known proprietor of the Randall House at Pulaski, whose long years of experience have taught him how to care for his guests to their best satisfaction, erected his hotel in the spring of 1894, on the site of the old Pulaski House. The location was well chosen since the hotel stands on a large plot of ground, ample in size for an extensive building, and where no other structures are crowded around it. This means light from all sides, an important desideratum for a big hotel. The building is three stories high, standing on Salina street and overlooking Salmon river. Broad covered verandas, well shaded by an abundance of woodbine, which Mrs. Randall has trained with her own hands and personally cared for and which gives the house a cool and inviting aspect in the hot days of summer, cover the entire front of the building.

The halls leading from the porches and entrance to all of the rooms on the three floors are broad and airy with high ceilings, and the whole interior of the house is kept neat and inviting by Mrs. Randall who personally looks after it, and her several experienced assistants.

The dining room, which is the first consideration of the travelling public, is a large, tidily kept room with broad, high windows in two sides looking out upon the gardens surrounding the house. Flower and vines trained upon the outside freshen the view of the diners and fill the room with a fragrant atmosphere. The tables are elaborately set, perfectly attended by skilled waiters, and the cuisine is temptingly prepared by the best of cooks.

The house throughout is modern in every appointment, being provided with natural gas and electricity for illuminating purposes and made comfortable in winter with steam heat.

Mr. Randall is a native of the town of Redfield and has been all of his life engaged in catering to the public, having been in the hotel business in several places, including Mexico, where he conducted the Mexico House three years. At one time he carried on a large summer hotel business at Mexico Point and became widely acquainted with a desirable class of summer visitors, many of whom stop with him at Pulaski every summer. His house enjoys a high reputation among the traveling men and is the headquarters for the large share of those who attend court and the delegates to political conventions which are held periodically in Pulaski.

The First Fire Engine.—On April 4, 1853, the village voted $200 for a fire engine. The new engine arrived in the village on Aug. 3. At the test which the fire company gave it, water was thrown 160 feet high. The Chief Engineer was R. Williams. The company was composed of 28 men. The foreman was F. Goodrich; first assistant foreman, B. Dow; second, P. Cropsy; bugleman, A. F. Mathewson; first assistant bugleman, A. H. Maltby; second assistant, bugleman, Eugene Lane; secretary, Charles Snow; treasurer, I. M. Hempstead; collector, Charles Crandall. The department then had altogether 600 feet of hose. The first service of the engine was at the fire which burned the barn of D. D. Tift, Jan. 12, 1854. The new engine house was opened on Thanksgiving day, 1869.

THE RANDALL HOUSE.

MRS. B. D. RANDALL.

The Randall Bazaar, a popular establishment which supplies the ladies of Pulaski and vicinity with the fashionable attire for which they are noted, was started two years ago. Mrs. Randall, an experienced milliner and costumer, had been engaged in the business up town for about twelve years, when she finally sold out to give her attention to the summer resort hotel at Mexico Point. Many of her old customers, however, as is common in such cases, thought that no one could serve them so well as one who had long furnished their wearing apparel, and in order to meet their demands Mr. Randell opened up the business placing his wife in charge of it. Her knowledge of the demands of the times and the people enables her to buy the latest and most fashionable goods and to trim after the newest styles. She at one time conducted a parlor millinery store at Mexico, but previously was the founder of the original Pulaski Bazaar. It is flattering to her ingenuity and good taste that she sets the patterns followed by others; and it has ever been her policy to procure good trimmers and keep them, paying them wages that are an inducement for them to remain, one having been with her for fifteen consecutive seasons. Her patronage is not confined to Pulaski as she has customers in Watertown and other places to whom she sends hats as the season requires. In connection with the millinery line she sells all kinds of ladies' furnishing goods, fancy goods, all kinds of embroidery and stamped goods, laces and the largest lines of children's bonnets and hats ever kept in town.

County Clerks.—James Adams (appointed), Oswego town., March 21, 1816; Joseph Davis (appointed), Oswego, March 19, 1818; Smith Dunlap (appointed), Sandy Creek, Feb. 19, 1821; Hiram Hubbell, Pulaski, term began Jan. 1, 1823; T. S. Morgan, Oswego, Jan. 1, 1826; Thomas C. Baker, Pulaski, Jan. 1, 1829; Erie Poor, Oswego, Jan. 1, 1832; Marinus W. Mathews, Pulaski, Jan. 1, 1835; Daniel H. Marsh, Oswego, Jan. 1, 1838; Andrew Z. McCarty, Pulaski, Jan. 1, 1841; John Carpenter, Oswego, Jan. 1, 1844; Jabez H. Gilbert, Pulaski, Jan. 1, 1847; Philander Rathbun, Oswego, Jan. 1, 1850; Edwin M. Hill, Pulaski, Jan. 1, 1853; Henry S. Conde, Hastings, Jan. 1, 1856; Samuel R. Taylor, Oswego, Jan. 1, 1859; Edward N. Rathbun, Oswego, Jan. 1, 1862; Bernice L. Doane, Pulaski, Jan. 1, 1865; Mannister Worts, Oswego, Jan. 1, 1868; John J. Stephens, Oswego town., Jan. 1, 1871; Brainard Nelson, Oswego, Jan. 1, 1874; Daniel E. Taylor, Granby, Jan. 1, 1877; Merrick Stowell, Oswego, Jan. 1, 1880; John Gardenier, Oswego, Jan. 1, 1883; John H. Oliphant, Oswego, Jan. 1, 1886; Thomas M. Costello, Albion, Jan. 1, 1889; William J. Pentelow, Fulton, Jan. 1, 1892; E. E. Frost, Oswego, Jan. 1, 1895; John S. Parsons, Oswego, Jan. 1, 1898; Frank M. Breed, Phœnix, Jan. 1, 1901.

Early Roads.—Among the earliest roads constructed in the county were Scriba's, from Rotterdam to Vera Cruz, and a plank road from Camden, Oneida county, to the same place. The latter passed through the towns of Amboy, Parish and Mexico. In 1806 a mail route was established between Onondaga and Oswego and a postoffice opened at the latter place. In 1807 a state road six rods wide was laid out from Onondaga Hill to the mouth of Ox Creek, in the present town of Granby, and thence to Oswego. A branch of this led from Ox Creek to Salina. In 1817 a post road was constructed between Oswego Falls and Rochester via the "Ridge road." In 1825 a road was built from Watertown to Syracuse, passing through the villages of Sandy Creek, Pulaski,

Huested, Photo. THE RANDALL BAZAAR.

Union Square, Colosse and Central Square. In 1816 Jacob L. Lazalere and James Geddes began the construction of a road from Oswego to Canandaigua via Hannibal, Sterling, Wolcott and Galen. In March, 1817, a company to build the Oswego Falls and Sodus Bay turnpike was incorporated, and in the same month the Oswego and Sodus branch turnpike was projected.

Pulaski Academy and Union Free School— The citizens of Pulaski, early in its history, showed an interest in the education of their children by maintaining public and private schools. For several years prior to 1853 the erection of an institution of higher learning was agitated and on the 4th day of June, 1853 an act was passed by the state legislature consolidating parts of three school districts lying within the village into one district to be known thereafter as the "Pulaski School District." Charles H. Cross, Hiram Murdock, Don A. King, George Gurley, Anson Maltby, Newton M. Wardwell, Anson R. Jones, Samuel Woodruff and William H. Lester were named as trustees and were empowered to establish a classi-

Abbie L. Green and Emma Beebee, preceptresses; G. L. Bragdon and J. F. Billiard, assistants. 1860 R. B. VanPatten and A. Hoose, principals; E. M. Desbrow, preceptress; J. F. Billiard, assistant. 1861–63 Pulaski E. Smith, principal; Emma Beebee, Lizzie P. Bush and Helen M. Rice, preceptresses; H. H. Butterworth and D. D. Owen, assistants. 1864 H. H. Butterworth, principal; Helen M. Rice, preceptress; D. D. Owen, assistant. 1865 H. H. Butterworth, N. White, M. B. Benton and J. W. Grant, principals; Mrs. H. H. Butterworth, preceptress; and J. W. Quinby, assistant. 1866 D. D. Owen, principal; Mrs. H. H. Butterworth, preceptress; N. B. Smith, assistant. 1867 N. B. Smith, principal; Kate J. Brown, preceptress; J. H. Mattison, assistant. 1868 H. W. Congdon, principal; Flora A. Potter, preceptress; E. Blanchard, assistant. 1869–79 S. Duffy, principal; Mrs. S. Duffy, preceptress; B. F. Miller, N. A. Wooster, W. Steele, R. L. Keyser, W. Archibald, H. W. Hunt, H. T. Hoyt, F. Gilman and S. C. Huntington, assistants. 1879–85 E. M. Wheeler, principal; Mary Lewis, Ida Bartlett, Lulu Pinkham and Elizabeth Nichols preceptresses; Misses Burns, Seager, Mrs. G. Skeel, Mr. Haggerty, Misses Kendal, Foote, and Porte assistants. 1886–87 J. M. Moore, principal; Mrs. J. M. Moore, R. M. Gilbert, preceptresses; B. M. Watson, Mr. Johnson and H. A. Brown, assistants. 1888 H. A. Brown, principal; R. M. Gilbert, preceptress; Minnie Burrill and Loretta O. Douglas, assistants. 1889 Jesse A. Ellsworth, principal; Grace King, preceptress; Grace Sisson and Carl Hartman, assistants. 1890–92 W. C. Gorman, principal; Mrs. W. C. Gorman, preceptress; A. L. Packard, D. L. Blaisdell, Miss Greene and Miss Crittendon, assistants. 1893–97 S. R. Shear, principal; Minnie Walker and S. Frances King, preceptresses;

BOARD OF EDUCATION.
Top Row (from left to right)—S. R. Trumbull, E. D. Forman, D. C. Dodge, G. F. Parsons. Lower Row (from left to right)—N. B. Smith, Secretary; I. G. Hubbs, D. C. Mahaffy, President; G. W. Douglas, S. C. Huntington.

cal school to be known as the Pulaski Academy. These men who founded our academy and contributed so much to the cause of higher education in this community are worthy of grateful remembrance. In April 1854 the beautiful grounds of the banks of the Salmon River were purchased and in the midst of the grove of chestnut, oak and maple trees the present commodious brick structure 80x50 feet and three stories high was erected at a cost of about $10,000. In the month of May of that year ground was first broken and the work progressed so rapidly under the direction of the building committee that on the 8th day of Jan., 1855 the building was accepted and dedicated with appropriate ceremonies. The dedicatory address was given by Hon. Henry M. Wright. The work of instruction was at once commenced with a large attendance of pupils from the village and surrounding towns. Stephen C. Miller was the first principal. The principals and instructors in the academic department have been as follows:—1855–56 S. C. Miller, Frances Baker, preceptress; Homer T. Fowler and J. W. Fenton, assistants. 1857–59 Henry L. Lamb, principal;

Alice Walker, Harriet S. Hollis, L. M. Ballister, Eva L. Miller, L. Grace Henderson, Mary E. Isham, and Grace Rich, assistants. 1898 G. M. Davison, principal; Elmer G. Bridgham, vice principal; S. Frances King, preceptress; L. Grace Henderson, Harriet S. Hollis, Frances C. Richardson and Lucy Ward, assistants. 1899–02 C. M. Bean, principal; Elmer G. Bridgham, Claude W. Klock and Leslie N. Broughton, vice principals; S. Frances King and L. Grace Henderson, preceptresses; Harriet S. Hollis, Frances C. Richardson, Ellen Beauchamp, Lena M. Chapman, Marion E. Wright and Annabel A. Hulburd, assistants.

In the transition from the old line academy largely independent of other schools to the modern high school as an integral part of the public school system Pulaski has kept pace with the development of American educational ideals. The old academy did a noble work and in the list of alumni are many honored names. However great its usefulness and standing may have been in the

PROF. CHARLES M. BEAN,
Principal of the Pulaski Union Free School.

past, in order to meet the increasing demands of popular education it was thought best to adopt the Union Free School system. Accordingly in 1892 an act was passed by the legislature repealing the charter of the old academy and it became a Union Free School, the academic department being retained and a small tuition being charged to non-resident pupils. The Pulaski High School with its excellent equipment of apparatus, its well selected and increasing library of 2,500 volumes, its experienced and efficient faculty is excelled by none in the state. It gives thorough preparation for college as well as for the professional and technical schools and the various occupations of life. The class that graduated in June, 1900, numbered 26, and 28 academic diplomas were credited to the school last year by the Regents in Albany. The teachers' training class has been an important feature for many years. Last year 19 training class certificates were secured by the Pulaski class. Upwards of 60 graduates from the class are now teaching in this and adjoining commissioners' districts. This fall seven Pulaski graduates enter college and as many more enter professional and business schools. The building has recently been thoroughly papered, painted and generally repaired at a large expense and the school rooms are very attractive. Faculty for the year 1902-03: Charles M. Bean, principal; Leslie N. Broughton,

vice principal; L. Grace Henderson, preceptress; Marion E. Wright, Carrie J. Eaton, Ellen Beauchamp and L. Grace Snyder, assistants; Anna C. Williams, senior department; Anna M. Lacy, junior department; Rose C. Fenton, intermediate and Zillah A. Rice, primary.

The officers of the Board of Education from its organization to he present time have been as follows: Presidents, George Gurley, Beeman Brockway, Sydney H. Tucker, Charles H. Cross, James N. Betts, George W. Woods, Rev. James Douglas, James W. Fenton, John F. Box, Andrew W. Dunn, Charles Tollner, L. J. Clark, M. L. Hollis and D C. Mahaffy; secretaries, Don A. King, Charles H. Cross, Lorenzo Ling, H. H. Lyman, Newton M. Thompson, Benj. Snow, A. A. Maltby, O. V. Davis, W. H. Austin, S. C. Huntington and N. B. Smith. The officers and members of the present board are as follows: D. C. Mahaffy, president; N. B. Smith, clerk; G. W. Douglas, D. C. Dodge, S. R. Trumbull, S. C. Huntington, I. G. Hubbs, E. D. Forman and G. E. Parsons.

Sheriffs.-- John S. Davis (appointed), Pulaski, March 21, 1816; Peter Pratt (appointed), Mexico, Feb. 4, 1820; Orris Hart (appointed), New Haven, Feb. 13, 1821; elected from Oswego, Jan. 1, 1823; Asa Dudley, Oswego town, Jan. 1, 1826; Hastings Curtiss, Hastings, Jan. 1, 1829; William Hale, Pulaski, Jan. 1, 1832; Jonathan Case, Fulton, Jan. 1, 1835; Jabez H. Gilbert, Orwell, Jan. 1, 1838; Norman Rowe, New Haven, Jan. 1, 1841; second term, Jan. 1, 1849; Marinus W. Matthews, Pulaski, Jan. 1, 1844; Horace J. Carey, Oswego, appointed to fill vacancy by death of Matthews, Dec. 5, 1844; Alvin Lawrence, Mexico, Jan. 1, 1846; George W. Stillman, Orwell, Jan. 1, 1852; Rufus Hawkins. Oswego, Jan. 1, 1855; Charles A. Perkins, Constantia, Jan. 1, 1858; Sidney M. Tucker, Pulaski, Jan. 1, 1861; re-elected from Oswego, Jan. 1, 1867; Robert D. Gillispie, Richland, Jan. 1, 1864; James Doyle, Oswego, Jan. 1, 1870; Henry H. Lyman, Pulaski, Jan. 1, 1873; Frank S. Low, Pulaski, Jan. 1, 1876; J. Lyman Bulkley, Sandy Creek, Jan. 1, 1879; Edwin L. Huntington, Mexico, Jan. 2, 1882;

Dunwick, Photo.   THE PULASKI UNION FREE SCHOOL.

Alfred N. Beadle, Pulaski, Jan. 1, 1885; John Van Buren, New Haven, Jan. 1, 1888; Amos Allport, Scriba, Jan. 1, 1891; Wilbur H. Selleck, Williamstown, Jan. 1, 1894; Wm. H. Enos, Scriba, Jan. 1, 1897; Albert Warren, Jan. 1, 1900.

The Charles Tollner's Sons Co. was established in 1864, at which time its founder, the late Charles Tollner, sr., engaged in the manufacture of floor tiling. Several months later he began the manufacture of smokers' pipes which were made of carbon composition. During the spring of 1875 Hier & Aldridge took the factory for the manufacture of cigar boxes, which continued but a short time when the United Paper Collar Co. of New York began the manufacture of boxes of various kinds. In 1879 the cabinet industry was added, the Clark Thread Co., being the contractors for a large part of the output of the factory. This enterprise was brought to a close by the fire of Jan. 14, 1885, which destroyed the entire plant.

Planing Mill and Lumber Yard.
CHARLES TOLLNER'S SONS CO.'S WORKS.

As an inducement to keep the factory in town the citizens of the village subscribed $5,000 to aid in rebuilding the works, with the result that inside of six months new and commodious buildings were constructed and equipped with machinery for turning out boxes of any size, style or description and in July, 1885, business was resumed.

After the death of Charles Tollner, sr., in 1897, his three sons organized the Charles Tollner's Sons Co., but in February, 1902, the plant and business passed into the hands of the present owners, Messrs. Richard W. Box, Albert F. Betts, Louis J. Clark and Irving G. Hubbs, who reorganized the company, retaining the same name. With the infusion of new life and abundant capital a new era for manufacturing came to Pulaski. The new proprietors are all Pulaski capitalists with the interests of Pulaski at heart. They are also men who have made a success of their respective callings, and who own considerable property in the village. The individual success of these gentlemen is a guarantee of the success of the company, which indeed is already an established fact.

Having organized the company and taken possession of the plant they at once laid plans to branch out in the manufacture of all kinds of boxes, to keep up with the times in their output and to increase their field of operations so that the works can be run throughout the year. From

time to time they have added new machinery and put on more help. They have been able to make some flattering contracts and today the enterprise stands on a footing with the best of its character, employing upwards of 125 people with a payroll of $800 a week. At the present time the company can supply promptly on order thread cabinets, viaticums, crokonole and bagatelle boards, counter trays, school companions, toy furniture and boxes of various kinds.

Factory Burned.—On the morning of Sept. 7, 1902, fire broke out in the south side or main building and that with the brick office and store room was entirely consumed, entailing a loss of about $50,000. As this work goes to press machinery is being placed in the north side buildings and plans for enlarging the same are being made so that work will, as soon as possible, be resumed.

Sons of Temperance.—Although there is no official record at hand we know that a Division of the Sons of Temperance existed in Pulaski at least half a century ago, for biographies of Revs. Salmon and Shipperd speak of their delivering lectures before the Sons of Temperance then. Dec. 22, 1873, another Division was organized in the M. E. church. The first officers were: W. P., Sidney T. Doane; W. A., Walter Meacham; R.S., John W.

Box and Cabinet Works.
CHARLES TOLLNER'S SONS CO.'S WORKS.

Richards; A. R. S., M. Antoinette Lyman; F. S., Lyman I. Robbins; treasurer, Mrs. S. T. Doane; chaplain, Rev. W. L. Tisdale; conductor, Fred Alexander; A. C., Mrs. W. Meacham; I. S., Mrs. M. Leffingwell; O. S., W. C. Wood. This Division retained its charter and did most excellent work until after the disastrous fire of the autumn of 1881, which destroyed not only their charter, but their entire property as well; which unfortunately was uninsured. The records of this Division contain many names familiar to the citizens of Pulaski. Some of the members are still with us. Some have found other homes and not a few have joined the ever increasing majority in the better country. Nov. 16, 1885, the present Division was organized by D. Lucas Huff, of Canada. This Division, although not attempting large things, has accomplished much good in a quiet way. It has not only helped some to reform, but what is quite as important, it has been through all these years, to very many members, a definite force in temperance training and education, whose power and value it is impossible to estimate. The present officers are: W. P., Rev. J. Foster Wilcox; W. A., Dr. C. H. Davis; R. S., Mary French; A. R. S., W. H. Dunwick; F. S., B. Snow; T., Mrs. B. Snow; chaplain, Alta M. Austin; conductor, C. D. Hadley; A. C., J. Morrison: sentinel, Mrs. Clara Runyon.

The Pulaski Bakery, which is located on the west side of Jefferson avenue and is conducted by Mr. Samuel J. Clyde, was established by a Mr. Blasher, May 15, 1893. The following September he disposed of his interest in the business to Mr.

1901 a one-story brick building was erected in the rear of the establishment and fitted up as a bake shop.

In connection with his business Mr. Clyde has a restaurant where light lunches are served. A complete line of confectionery constantly in stock.

Mr. Clyde has a bakery wagon in connection with his plant, and besides a city route visits all the summer resorts along the lake during the season.

Mr. Clyde is an experienced and skillful baker and also employs a first-class baker the year round.

Mr. Samuel J. Clyde was born in Ogdensburg,

Huested, Photo.
S. J. Clyde (Dunwick)
The Salesroom (Huested).

S. J. CLYDE'S BAKERY.

The Bakery (Huested.)
Mrs. S. J. Clyde (Dunwick)

J. J. Wade, who conducted the place for several months. Mr. Clyde, the present proprietor, purchased of Mr. Wade his interest in the business in October, 1895. After making extensive improvements to the place Mr. Clyde reopened the bakery Nov. 16, 1895, and has conducted the baking business since that time. A few years ago he added a large and complete stock of fancy groceries. Under Mr. Clyde's skillful management the business has continued to grow and trade increased so rapidly that more room was needed for the conducting of his extensive business. In

N. Y., June 5, 1869. He was united in marriage to Miss Mina Wood, of Ogdensburg, June 5, 1893. They have three children, Mary J., Ray D. and J. Edward.

The First County Officers were commissioned by a council of appointment and were as follows: First judge, Barnet Mooney; associate judges, Henry Williams, Smith Dunlap, Peter D. Hugunin, David Easton and Edmund Hawkes; assistant justice, Daniel Hawkes, jr.; surrogate, Elias Brewster; county clerk, James Adams; sheriff, John S. Davis.

LEOPOLD JOH.

Leopold Joh, proprietor of the famous summer hotel at Selkirk-on-the-Lake, has, during the few years he has been there, made that a favorite resort for summer visitors. Selkirk is a small village on the north shore of Salmon river and the east shore of Lake Ontario. Here stands the old government light house which was in government service from 1838 to 1858. To-day it belongs to Mr. Joh, who, from May 1 to November 1, keeps the light burning for the benefit of those who desire to sail on the lake. A few yards from the light house, with a broad sandy beach between the building and the water, stands the light house hotel, erected by Mr. Joh in 1899, consequently a new building with all modern comforts. From the broad porches that extend across the front, his guests have an unobstructed view of the lake. In the dining room, seated at the tables, while regaling themselves with the delicacies of the season, they have this charming view spread out before them. During the hot days there is always a breeze from the open lake which neither cove or headland obstructs, and which sweeps across the porches and through the open windows, bringing a cooling relief. The cool evenings are made comfortable by heaters in which is burned natural gas, also used for cooking.

Every season this place is becoming more popular, many guests from New York, Baltimore, Oswego and Syracuse being regular visitors. Carriages take them to and from the trains at Pulaski over a level drive of only three miles. Or they may come in by boat from various points on the lake; Oswego, twenty-six miles west; Kingston, forty miles north or Sackets and Henderson Harbors, respectively fourteen and twenty miles distant.

Selkirk occupies the lake shore of what is popularly known as Port Ontario. The latter is a village a half mile up the Salmon river on the opposite shore. It is on the main line of steamers which pass from the various ports on the Great Lakes to the St. Lawrence river and its fashionable summer resorts. From Selkirk, if one does not care to go by water, he can make a trip to the Thousand Islands on the fast trains of the New York Central, which in the season daily pass from Syracuse to the north. Selkirk, and Mr. Joh's hotel, which is really the only summer hotel there, have many other attractions besides what have been mentioned.

The mouth of the Salmon river with its numerous shoals and channels, affords excellent black bass fishing, many of which are caught off the dock of the hotel. Besides, in the lake are an abundance of pickerel and perch and for years white fish have been caught in great numbers. There is also good duck hunting in the fall. Guests who desire may take one day's excursion inland to some of the best speckled trout streams in Northern New York. Sail and row boats are to be had at the hotel. The land scenery is charming, there being just across the river a well known picnic grove.

In the seventeenth century it was the rendezvous of the Iroquois Indians, and the French Jesuits resorted here on several notable occasions. The site of one of the most notable conferences between the French and Iroquois is but a stone's throw from the hotel, within plain view of its porches. Among other historic spots near by are Texas Point, five miles away, Stony Island, twenty-one miles, and Sandy Creek, the latter a stream made famous by the battle between the British under Col. Yoe and the Americans in the war of 1812.

Mr. Joh is an experienced caterer and knows

LIGHT HOUSE HOTEL, LEOPOLD JOH, Proprietor, Selkirk-on-the-Lake, (Port Ontario) N. Y.

well how to entertain his guests. Seeing the advantages of Selkirk for a summer home, he wisely bought a considerable tract here and the success he has met with has confirmed his good judgment. He was born in Heidelberg, Baden, Germany, November 23, 1838, and came to New York city in 1865. In 1866 he removed to Syracuse where he lived until he came to Selkirk in 1895. His son ably assists in the conduct of the hotel, which between them has been made one of the best resorts on the lake.

Port Ontario is Historic.—This beautiful outlook on Lake Ontario, the historical name of which is La Famine, occupies a more prominent place in the annals of early colonization, and especially in the contests between the French and the Iroquois or Five Nations for control of their lands than many superficial readers of history are aware. It was here that war parties from both sides rendezvoused on their canoe journeyings between the mouth of the Oswego river and Fort Frontenac (Kingston, Ont.) for the purpose of replenishing their supplies which they were generally able to do, the Salmon river where it empties into the lake usually furnishing an abundance of fish then as it does now. To-day it is regarded as one of the best black bass grounds. Formerly, however, salmon trout were caught in abundance, though considerably farther up stream. Between thirty and forty miles from its mouth the Oneidas annually visited the river to procure their winter supply of salmon. At one time a great city was projected at Port Ontario. The government erected a light house, which was afterwards abandoned and is still standing, being now occupied by Mr. Joh, the proprietor of a summer hotel. The contemplated city was surveyed and platted and streets were laid out on paper. On April 10, 1837, the Port Ontario Hydraulic Company was incorporated with a cash capital of $100,000, its purpose being the construction of "a canal from the falls below Pulaski to the village of Port Ontario, along the banks of Salmon river." This was intended to supply Port Ontario with water power. On April 27, 1871, the Salmon River Improvement Company, capitalized at $50,000, was incorporated for the purpose of clearing the river channel so that logs could be floated down. But a proposed government appropriation which gave life to the project of a city that was expected to rival all other ports on the great lakes, never materialized, and to-day the place is the site of two small hamlets, separated by the river, that called Selkirk being a summer resort on the north shore of the river and close to the lake, and the oldest of the two known as Port Ontario, a small agricultural settlement across the river, a short distance back from the lake.

State Officers.—William F. Allen, Oswego, Controller, from Jan. 1, 1868, to June, 1870, when he was elected Judge of the Court of Appeals. John Cochran, Oswego, Attorney-General, 1864–'5. Henry H. Lyman, Pulaski, Commissioner of Excise, 1896–1901 (died while in office); succeeded by P. W. Cullinan, of Oswego, in 1901. Henry Fitzhugh, Oswego, Canal Commissioner, 1851–'7. Gilson A. Dayton, Mexico, Canal Auditor, 1871–'4; John A. Place, Oswego, Canal Auditor, appointed May 20, 1880, and held the office until it was abolished, March 1, 1883.

La Barre at La Famine, Sept. 5, 1684.—On July 10, 1684, La Barre, the French Governor of Canada, left Quebec with 700 Canadians, 130 regular French soldiers and 200 Mission Indians, beating against the currents of the St. Lawrence river in unwieldy flat boats and frail birch bark canoes. After several days of wearisome labors they entered what is now the harbor of Kingston, Ont., seeking rest and safety behind the palisades of Fort Frontenac, the extreme fortified outpost of the French at that time. La Barre, the Governor of Néw France, as Canada was then called, who was in personal command of the expedition, in a letter to the French court, thus relates the object of the journey: "My purpose is to exterminate the Senecas; for otherwise your Majesty need take no further account of this country, since there is no hope of peace with them, except when they are driven to it by force." Not daring to meet the Senecas in council, La Barre sent the Jesuit Le Moyne to ask mediation of the Onondagas, and appointed as a meeting place the mouth of the Salmon river. While waiting to hear from his embassy, La Barre kept his party in camp under the protection of the guns of the fort, where in the heat of August they sickened and died by scores. Provisions, too, became scarce, and when finally on the first of September the expedition crossed the lake and pitched its encampment on the sandy tongue of land which forms the north shore of the river where it empties into the lake, the men were suffering terribly from lack of food. Two days later Le Moyne, accompanied by Big Mouth, the famous Onondaga chief, and thirteen of their wisest sachems, arrived, attended by a large retinue of Indians. That well known fishing resort on the east shore of Ontario lake, now in the midst of a populous people, two or three miles from the village of Pulaski, never before or since presented such a scene of savage glory—such picturesque groupings of wilderness finery. There were assembled the great warriors of the Iroquois, the fiercest tribe on the continent. Under the banners of France, led by the King's own representative, the Governor of New France, who representing the most brilliant court of those times, made all the display of pomp and power that his environments and methods of traversing a new country permitted, were assembled the chevaliers seeking wealth and adventure in the new world; gathered from the west even to the shores of Lake Superior under their chieftains, Du Lhut and La Durantaye, came the French-Canadian Indian fighters and hunters, whose lives were spent in roaming the forests, dressed in their strange costumes of skins, known in story and song as the coureurs de bois; in their rude encampments, partly hidden in the scrub and timber that then skirted the banks of the Salmon river, were the red allies of the French—all of them hunted by the Iroquois, of whom they were in deadly fear. There were the Abenakis, the terrors of the New England colonists, from the coasts of Maine and Massachusetts; the Algonquins, from the remote Canadian interiors; the Hurons, from the shores of Lake Huron, and the converted Iroquois, whom the Jesuits had gathered in their missions scattered through Canada, from Quebec to the lakes. The most effeminate power of the civilized world was there in that little corner of a great wilderness, cooped up in their tents, pitched on the sand heaps, to meet in solemn treaty the representatives of a fierce and barbarous nation of Indians. Who of all the hundreds of pleasure seekers that annually visit that cool and invigorating spot, know anything of the historic associations that are attached to it? On that hot September day; two centuries ago, nearly a thousand of this strange assortment of peoples gathered to a feast of bread, wine and salmon trout. It was the fourth of the month, and on the morrow the two powers, the French and the Iroquois, were to determine which could outwit the other in their game for the control of the American continent.

The average historian has never made much of that meeting at the mouth of the Salmon river. But it is the fact that it was one of the most momentous of colonial history. The French held in alliance all of the Indian nations of the eastern part of America which at that time were inimical to the welfare of the white races then trying to get a foothold on the Western Continent. except the Iroquois. The latter then held the leverage of power between the English and French, dickering with both without giving either the opportunity to

OFF SELKIRK-ON-THE-LAKE, (PORT ONTARIO,) LAKE ONTARIO.

gain any advantage. As between the two, it is true, they were friendly to the English, but even they, the Iroquois, were holding at arm's length, so to speak, and at the same time threatening the French with destruction, having already conquered all of the Indian tribes who could possibly be a factor in the race for the possession of the new continent. The situation to the French had finally become unendurable. The Governor had written to the French King that the Iroquois must be severely punished or the Court of Versailles must give up the scheme of colonizing America. So with all the bluster of which he was capable La Barre had left his capital to settle the momentous question once and forever. He had gathered his entire fighting strength on this side of the Atlantic, and had got as far as the Iroquois outposts. There he evidently determined to once more resort to diplomacy. His fever for war suddenly subsided. The last cast of the dice was to be made at La Famine. The Onondagas, the rulers of the confederacy had previously refused to take a single step towards treating for peace, and

even after Onontio (as they called the French Governor) had come as far as Frontenac to meet them in a council they had refused to cross the lake for a conference, and haughtily demanded that the council fire should be moved into their territory, saying that they would condescend to go as far as the limits of their fishing grounds, and no farther.

So on this third of September here they were— both parties to the controversy—the red demons their hands reeking with the blood of the defenceless people they had but recently massacred within sight of the parapets of Quebec, and the almost starved remnant of the western armies of France. A duel royal of diplomats was to settle the fate of France—yes, of nations, since if the Iroquois were outgeneraled, the contest for their lands would be quickly settled between the English and French, the latter moving by the hundreds into the Iroquois territory, where, as it turned out, they were never able to settle even a corporal's guard.

The morning of the fifth opened bright. All ceremonials the Iroquois delighted in, their sachem observed as they 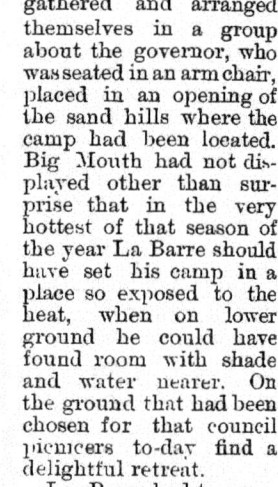 gathered and arranged themselves in a group about the governor, who was seated in an arm chair, placed in an opening of the sand hills where the camp had been located. Big Mouth had not displayed other than surprise that in the very hottest of that season of the year La Barre should have set his camp in a place so exposed to the heat, when on lower ground he could have found room with shade and water nearer. On the ground that had been chosen for that council picnicers to-day find a delightful retreat.

La Barre had two reasons for selecting the camp he did. He mistrusted the Iroquois, and had good reason for so doing, and his force was in such a helpless condition that he desired concealment of the actual situation so far as possible. The elevation of his camp with the lake shore partly surrounding it, favored both purposes. The Iroquois were not known to violate treaty ground, although they were vile dissimulators and had no compunctions about breaking treaties. But La Barre well knew that they had not forgotten the avowed object of his expedition, and he felt safer situated where he could look down upon their camp rather than they upon his Before the Onondaga delegation had arrived he had sent home all of his sick men in order further to conceal his weakness. Supposing he had succeeded in keeping them ignorant of his crippled forces, what must have been his surprise when Big Mouth in his insolent reply to the commander's firm demands, said that he saw Onontio, "raving in a camp of sick men."

The council opened with the two parties seated, in Indian fashion. La Barre began, say his Jesuit chroniclers, with a demand for satisfaction and indemnity on the part of the Iroquois for the massacreing that had been going on, saying that in case of refusal his king had order him to declare war. Then he complained that the Five Nations had "introduced the English into the lakes which belonged to the king, my master, and among the tribes who are his children, in order to destroy the trade of his subjects, and seduce these people from the obedience they owe him."

The reply of Big Mouth is characteristic of the man. "Onontio," said he, "when you left Quebec, you must have thought that the heat of the sun had burned the forests that make our country inaccessable to the French, or that the lake had overflowed them so that we could not escape from our villages. Now your eyes are opened; for I and my warriors have come to tell you that the Senecas, Cayugas, Onondagas, Oneidas and Mohawks are all alive. Listen, Onontio, I am not asleep. My eyes are open and by the sun that gives me light I see a great captain at the head of a band of soldiers, who talks like a man in a dream. I see Onontio raving in a camp of sick men, whose lives the Great Spirit has saved by smiting them with disease. Our women had snatched war clubs, and our children and old men seized bows and arrows to attack your camp, if our warriors had not restrained them, when your messenger, Akouessan (Le Moyne) appeared in our village."

In the afternoon a second session was held at which terms of peace were agreed upon—a peace which the Iroquois broke before the French had got back to Montreal. But the latter were too depleted in numbers to do more than defend themselves behind their barricades and the country of the Iroquois which they had looked upon with covetous eyes, they were never able to occupy. Their failure at the peace conference at La Famine to impress the Iroquois with their might and power had placed them in the lowest estimate of the Five Nations who no longer feared or respected them and the result was that not only did their enemies, the Iroquois, at once declare their fealty to the English whom they thereafter called father instead of brother, but it thoroughly alienated from the French their western red allies who became convinced that the French were powerless to defend them against the mighty Iroquois, with whom they at once sought conciliation and peace. The last cast of the dice made at the mouth of the Salmon River bereft the French of the last hope of getting a foothold south of the great lakes and a vast region which became Anglicized without their opposition otherwise might have become in reality a new France.

The Woman's Foreign Missionary Society of the Methodist church was organized Dec. 31, 1872, under the pastorate of Rev. Wm. Watson by Bishop J. T. Peck. Its charter members numbered fourteen. The work of the society has been to engage and unite the efforts of christian women in sending female missionaries to foreign fields, and in supporting them and native christian teachers and bible readers in those fields. Its first president was Mrs. Louisa S. Allen, who served the society with energy and faithfulness eight years, when on account of failing health, she retired. At her death she left the society a bequest of $500. The second president was Mrs. Celia Box, a woman of strong traits of character. Her decision and energy went far toward shaping and directing the work; her liberality placed many dollars in the treasury, and thus spread the good news in heathen lands. She served thirteen years, when from age and infirmities she laid down the work and went to her reward. Mrs. O. Clark, Mrs. C. Brooks and Mrs. N. Hunt each served one year. The acting president has served seven years. The membership of the society is now forty-one; receipts for the past year, $95. Total receipts since organized, $1603.72. Officers: President, Mrs. Oscar Clark; first vice president, Mrs. S. O. Barnes; recording secretary, Miss Ellen Orr; corresponding secretary, Miss Rosetta Coit; treasurer, Mrs Alice Rogers.

The Woman's Home and Foreign Missionary Society.—A number of ladies of the First Baptist church society met in the conference room of the church on Friday, Sept. 10, 1875, and organized The Woman's Baptist Missionary Society. The following officers were elected: President, Mrs. Baker; secretary, Mrs. E. W. Peckham; treasurer, Mrs. C. Leffingwell. At the next annual meeting Mrs. M. B. Comfort was elected president and Mrs. Gurley vice president. After the departure of Rev. and Mrs. Comfort from the village few meetings were held until the coming of Rev. and Mrs. J. J. Townsend. Mrs. Townsend was elected president. The next officers of the society were Mrs. D. D. Owen, president, and Mrs. J. W. Fenton, vice president. About this time a public service was held in the form of a farewell service to Miss Anna Wall, who went to prepare herself for the life of a missionary. Mrs. D. D. Owen continued as the faithful president of the society until 1890. Upon her resignation, Mrs. L. R. Muzzy was elected president and Mrs. A. A. Clifford, vice president. Rev. I. N. Steelman succeeded Rev. D. D. Owen as pastor and gave encouragement to the society. Later he and Mrs. Steelman went as home missionaries to Mexico. Mrs. W. C. Peck was elected president to succeed Mrs. Muzzy. Mrs. E. W. Peckham called a meeting of the society and inaugurated a study of Baptist missions. Mrs. D. J. Bailey succeeded Mrs. Peckham as president and Mrs. D. D. Potter was elected vice president. Mrs. Potter acted as president after the removal of Rev. and Mrs. Bailey until the coming of Rev. and Mrs. J. Foster Wilcox. Mrs. Wilcox was elected president and Mrs. Frank Wilder vice president. Faithful secretaries who have served the society are, Mrs. C. Leffingwell, Miss Marion Peckham, Mrs. L. R. Muzzy, Mrs. Benjamin Snow, Miss Lora E. Watson, Miss Belle Bragdon, Miss S. Ellen Hadley, Mrs. S. A. Richards, Miss Margaret Weed and Mrs. H. J. Howlett. The officers are: President, Mrs. Wilcox; vice president, Mrs J. L. Hutchens; secretary, Mrs. H. J. Howlett; treasurer, Mrs. John F. Andrews.

State Senators from Oswego County—Alvin Bronson, 1823-4, '30-3; Avery Skinner, Mexico, 1838-41; Enoch B. Talcott, Oswego, 1845-6 (his term was cut short by an amendment to the constitution); Thomas H. Bond, Oswego, 1848-9; Moses P. Hatch, Oswego, 1851; James Platt, Oswego, 1852-3; M. Lindley Lee, Fulton, 1856-7; Cheney Ames, Oswego, 1858-9, '64-5; Andrew S. Warner, Pulaski, 1860 1; Richard K. Sanford, Fulton, 1862-3; John J. Wolcott, Volney, 1866-7; Abner C. Mattoon, Oswego, 1868-9; William Foster, Constantia, 1872-3; Benjamin Doolittle, Oswego, 1876-7; George B. Sloan, Oswego, 1886-'91; Nevada N. Stranahan, Fulton, 1896-1902.

COUNT PULASKI,
After Whom the Village was Named.

The Woman's Home Missionary Society of the M. E. church was organized by Miss Amelia A. Morris, Feb. 11, 1887, with ten charter members. The following officers were elected: President, Miss Amelia A. Morris; vice presidents, Miss Harriet Hollis, Miss Julia Wood, and Miss Grace Becker; recording secretary, Miss Kate Lamb; corresponding secretary, Miss Adele Jones; executive committee, Miss Flora E. Morris, Miss Ritta Seamans and Miss Kate Brown. The society is auxiliary to the Woman's Home Missionary Society of the Methodist Episcopal church which has for its missionary field the United States and all its new possessions. The total amount of money sent to the general treasurer is $478; and supplies sent to frontier ministers and Industrial Homes in the south, $780. On March 12, 1902, the society celebrated its fifteenth anniversary with a membership of sixty-four, at which time the following officers were elected: President, Mrs. John Y. Mahaffy; vice presidents, Mrs. Silas W. Holmes, Miss Cora A. Hunt and Mrs. D. C. Dodge; recording secretary, Mrs. Ernest Potter; corresponding secretary, Mrs. W. S. Rogers; treasurer, Mrs. C. H. Davis.

The Young Woman's Home Missionary Society of the First Methodist Episcopal church was organized, Aug. 16, 1900, by Mrs. N. W. Bass, conference organizer, with a membership of twenty-five. Meetings are regularly held on the third Friday evening of each month, at the homes of the members. The last meeting of the year is celebrated by a banquet with toasts and other speeches and song. The last annual banquet occurred Friday evening, March 28, 1902, in the parlors of the church, some thirty friends being especially invited. After the toasts, songs and music by the orchestra, games enlivened the occasion. The work of the society has been as follows: In 1900 supplies valued at $11 were sent to Ritter Home, Athens, Tenn. During 1901, $5 was sent toward the support of a colored girl in Kent Home in Greensboro, N. C.; and supplies valued at $10 have been sent to the Immigrant Home in New York City. The officers elected for the year 1902, are: Directress, Mrs. S. O. Barnes; president, Miss Grace McBratney; first vice president, Miss Kate Haggerty; second vice president, Miss

Carrie Greenwood; third vice president, Miss Lela Stowell; recording secretary, Miss Harriet Lane; corresponding secretary, Miss Lou Robbins; treasurer, Miss Mary Ehle.

The Railroads of the County.—The Oswego & Utica Railroad Company was chartered, May 13, 1836, but it did nothing for several years. On April 20, 1839, the Oswego & Syracuse RR. Co. was incorporated, the road being completed in October, 1848. The Rome & Watertown Railroad Company was chartered in 1832. Work was begun at Rome in November, 1848, and in May, 1851, the road was constructed as far as Pierrepont Manor. The Oswego & Rome Railroad Company constructed a road from Oswego to Richland station via Pulaski and Mexico in the fall of 1865. The Oswego Midland Railroad Company was incorporated Jan. 11, 1866. The road, extending from Oswego to Jersey City, a distance of 325 miles, was completed in 1872. It is now known as the New York, Ontario & Western railroad. The Syracuse Northern Railroad Company was chartered in 1870 and on the 18th of May in the same year construction was begun. The road was opened, Nov. 9, 1871. It is now a part of the Rome, Watertown & Ogdensburg system, leased by the New York Central & Hudson River Railroad Company, and extends from Syracuse to Pulaski; where it connects with the Oswego and Mexico branch of the same system. The Lake Ontario Shore railroad also a part of that system, was constructed in 1871, connecting Oswego with Lewiston on the Niagara river. A branch road, extending from Woodard, a station on the Syracuse Northern railroad to Fulton and there connecting with the New York, Ontario & Western railroad, gives the New York Central entrance to Oswego direct from Syracuse. The R., W. & O. system was leased to the New York Central in March, 1891.

Samuel Bragdon, aged 90 years, died in Pulaski, Nov. 22, 1852, the last revolutionary soldier in the town.

Court House.

THE COUNTY BUILDINGS IN 1860.

The Ladies' Aid Society of the Baptist church was organized about the year 1835, by the ladies of the church and society. Its meetings were held at the homes of the members and in the parlors of the church. A continuous record has not been kept. The president of the society was usually the pastor's wife. Some of the other presidents were Mrs. Benjamin Snow, Mrs. Loren Champney, Mrs. George Gurley, Mrs. Adnoriam Fisher, Mrs. George Peckham, Mrs. Joseph Wood, Mrs. Charles Calkins and Mrs. William Graham. April 11, 1883, the ladies of the society met at the parsonage to reorganize under the name of the Ladies' Benevolent Society. A new constitution and by-laws were adopted and the following officers elected: President, Mrs. J. W. Fenton; vice president, Mrs. E. M. Fisher; secretary, Miss Belle Bragdon; treasurer, Mrs. R. S. Avery. Since 1884 the officers have been as follows: 1884—President, Mrs. H. V. Harbottle; vice president, Mrs. E. M. Peckham; secretary, Miss Belle Bragdon; treasurer, Miss Marion Peck am. 1885—President, Mrs. L. R. Muzzy; first vice president, Mrs. D. D. Owen; second vice president, Mrs. J. W. Fenton; secretary, Miss Lenora Richards; treasurer, Mrs. Frank Rickard. 1886—President, Mrs. Willis C. Peck; first vice president, Mrs. N. A. Peckham; second vice president, Mrs. D. D. Owen; secretary, Miss Margaret Weed; treasurer, Miss Lenora Richards. 1887—President, Mrs. E. M. Peckham; vice president, Mrs. L. R. Muzzy; secretary, Miss Margaret Weed; treasurer, Mrs. H. V. Harbottle. 1888—President, Mrs. James Eaton; vice president, Mrs. H. V. Harbottle; secretary, Mrs. Willis C. Peck; treasurer, Miss Marion Peckham. 1889—President, Mrs. Benjamin Snow; vice president, Mrs. Willis C. Peck; secretary, Miss Marion Peckham; treasurer, Mrs. N. W. Peckham. 1890—President, Mrs. Benjamin Snow; vice president, Mrs. Albert F. Betts; secretary, Miss Margaret Weed; treasurer, Miss Lenora Richards. 1891—President, Mrs. D. D. Potter; vice president, Mrs. Willis C. Peck; secretary, Miss Margaret Weed; treasurer, Miss Lenora Richards. 1892—President, Mrs. D. D. Potter; vice president, Miss Eva Pierce; secretary, Mrs. George Washington; treasurer, Miss Lenora Richards. 1893—President, Mrs. L. R. Muzzy; vice president, Miss Eva Pierce; secretary, Mrs. R. E. Thompson; treasurer, Miss Lenora Richards. 1898—President, Mrs. James Eaton; vice president, Miss Laura Roberts; secretary, Mrs. Benjamin Snow; treasurer, Mrs. Albert F. Betts. 1900—President, Mrs. D. D. Potter; vice president, Miss Laura Roberts; secretary, Mrs. Frank Wilder; treasurer, Mrs. Albert F. Betts; 1901—President, Mrs. Benjamin Snow; vice president, Mrs. Almon Champney; secretary, Mrs. Frank Wilder; treasurer, Mrs. Albert F. Betts. 1902—President, Mrs. John Andrews; vice president, Mrs. Harlan Howlett; secretary, Mrs. J. L. Hutchens; treasurer, Mrs. Albert F. Betts. During the year of 1901, under the auspices of this society, the bi-weekly thimble party was inaugurated and has proven to be an interesting feature of the work.

Early Landlords.—Benjamin Winch in 1804 located in Pulaski and opened his house for the accommodation of travelers. Strangers were rare in those days and the accommodations of a private house were sufficient to accommodate all who came that way. But as more settlers came in, the usual privileges of the tavern were demanded and in 1807, J. A. Matthewson erected a structure for that purpose just north of the site now occupied by the Pulaski House. Three years later, 1810, a better building was put up by Mr. Matthewson on the adjoining site and a hotel has stood there ever since. In 1829 a large addition, the main part of the hotel, was erected. The landlords of this house succeeding Matthewson were E. Young, Silas Harmon, Anson Maltby, Robert Kelly, Dr. Lewis, J. A. Matthewson, from 1840 to 1863; Joseph Curtis, Huggins & Taylor, Mr. Baldwin, Mr. Helmer, N. Johnson, Mr. Stacy, W. H. Gray, G. L. Hubbs, S. A. Palmer and Mr. Van Patten. The old Pulaski House, formerly the Palmer House, under the proprietorship of S. A. Palmer, was destroyed by fire, March 11, 1890. Other taverns were Brainard's Hotel, Levy Brainard, proprietor, changed to the Salmon River House in 1849, by J. A. Ford, landlord; Pulaski Temperance House, corner of Jefferson and Furnace streets, Henry Emmerson, proprietor; the California House, O. B. Macy, proprietor; Eagle Tavern, A. McLean, and The Randall House, B. D. Randall.

Fish Protection in the Salmon.—It was not many years after the white man came that the supply of salmon in that river began to decline rapidly. Often trouble broke out between the settlers and their red neighbors, the Indians, as the result of their efforts to compel the latter to keep away from certain parts of the stream in which owners of contiguous territory considered they had the best right to fish. It was useless to expect to get fish as long as the Indians were permitted to make their annual forays, since they gave no room for any one else to approach the stream. Such was the common way of expressing the situation. At last the settlers "arose in their might," and an appeal to the legislature gave them some relief. On April 3, 1818, the wanton destruction of fish was prohibited by law. This was supplemented on May 4, 1835, by an act requiring the construction of fishways in dams. A short time after, the supervisors of Oswego county took up the matter, and on De·. 13, 1849, enacted a measure prohibiting the catching of salmon with any seine, weir or trap within one mile from the mouth of Salmon river, between April 30 and Oct. 20. The legislature on May 12, 1875, passed an act which prohibited the spearing and netting of salmon in the Salmon river between Salmon River falls and the lake. Eventually the salmon disappeared. They were succeeded, however, by black bass, which during favorable seasons, when the water is not too high, are caught in considerable numbers and of fair size, in the river below Pulaski. In fact along the shoals, starting from the lower dam, within the corporation limits, this species of gamey fish may be caught anywhere on the river to the lake.

County Treasurers.—Peter Pratt, Mexico, 1816; Elias Brewster, Mexico, 1820; Avery Skinner, Mexico, 1827; Robert A. Stitt, 1839; Starr Clark, 1840; Hiram Walker, 1846; Samuel H. Stone, Mexico, 1849; Henry C. Peck, Mexico, 1855; Luther H. Conklin, Mexico, 1858; John Dowdle, Oswego, 1879; George Goodier, Oswego, 1882 (died in office in 1886, the first year after his re-election); E. Eugene McKinstry, Oswego, (appointed by the supervisors in Goodier's place) February, 1886; Thomas Moore, Oswego, 1886, re-elected 1889 and again every term since.

View on West Side of Jefferson St, Pulaski.

A PART OF THE BUSINESS SECTION, 1860.

The First Plank Road in the United States was built between Central Square and Syracuse and was opened in July 1846. The Rome and Oswego Plank Road Company was organized in 1847 and was completed the following year. It passed through Scriba, New Haven, Mexico, Albion and Williamstown. This was one of the most important thoroughfares for through passengers from the east to the west before the railroads were opened across the state. Passengers then came by rail as far as Rome, the western terminus of the railroads, thence by stage coach to Oswego and from there on west via the lakes. The Syracuse & Oswego plank road between Liverpool and Oswego, was begun in 1848, a road being already in operation between that village and Syracuse. The Hannibal and Sterling plank road was built about the same time, connecting at the latter place with the plank road for Oswego. In 1857 daily stage lines were operated between Oswego and Pulaski, Oswego and Kasoag, Oswego and Auburn and Oswego and Richland Station, while a tri-weekly line ran from Oswego to Rochester.

Mrs. Orrin Beadle has resided in the village of Orwell since 1855, and the pretty and well cared for residence she now occupies has been her home since about 1865 or '66. Her husband was one of two brothers who for several years engaged largely in dairying, on a farm one mile south of the village, on what is known as the Salmon River road. It was always known as the H. and O. Beadle farm. It passed out of the hands of the family in 1872 or '73. When Mr. and Mrs. Orrin Beadle moved into the village, they purchased and occupied the block just east of her present home. But about 1861 or early in the beginning of the war, they were burned out, and it was four years later that they bought and occupied the house and grounds where Mrs. Beadle now lives.

The Novelty Works at Orwell, W. H. Lattimer & Sons, proprietors, was established five years ago in the same place by the present firm, which consists of the father, W. H. Lattimer, and his sons, Stanley, John, George and Harry. From a small beginning, started by the senior member chiefly to give his sons a good business, it has grown to be one of the important industries of the village. Mr. Lattimer had been running a planing mill for twenty-five years, and is widely and well known throughout this section. The old planing mill was reconstructed to accommodate the new business. The building, which is comparatively new, is 50 by 70 feet, two floors, and the machinery is run by 25-horse power engine. During the busy season fifteen or twenty hands are employed. The product of the factory consists of step-ladders, lawn swings, a general line of summer porch goods, including a half dozen different chairs. The goods are shipped into all sections of the east.

View on West Side of Jefferson St, Pulaski.

WELL KNOWN OLD STRUCTURES, 1860.

Orwell is one of the prettiest villages in Oswego county. It is a no-license town, having been sixty years since liquor was allowed to be sold within the town. Although situated two and one-half miles from the railroad it is a place where considerable trade and manufacturing is carried on. Located in the midst of a good dairy and farming country its trade comes largely from a well-to-do class of farmers. The few stores in the village are much superior in every way to many in the more pretentious villages elsewhere, and the residences are generally kept in good order, making pleasant, commodious homes. Factories, together with the usual grist and saw-mills, several creameries and cheese factories, give employment to more than a hundred people from the surrounding country. The Woodbury chair works a prosperous industry which turns out a large production every year. W. H. Lattimer & Sons' novelty works is another prominent institution of the village, which manufactures the best goods in

a place of about 500 inhabitants. The first store was opened there about 1830 by Alvin Strong, although about the same time Gilbert & Decker were engaged at the corners in trade. In 1840 Orimell B. Olmstead engaged in trade, and continued until 1874, when his son, A. E. Olmstead, succeeded him in the business which he is still conducting. Also at the present time are the following stores: Charles Babcock Albert House and E. S. Beecher; the blacksmith shops of Ira S. Platt, Clayton Platt and James Phillips. Orwell was first designated as Moscow, but through the influence of John Reynolds, the first supervisor of the town, the post-office was officially named Orwell, from the fact that it was the principal trading place of the town, and of course the same name was attached to the village. About 1835 Reuben Salisbury built the first grist-mill in the village. Three years later a small tannery was erected by Orrin Weston. In 1854 it was purchased and enlarged by Weston & Lewis, who rebuilt the structure after the fire in August, 1862. Lane, Pierce & Co., of Boston,

Messenger, Photo.   VIEWS OF ORWELL, N. Y.
Four Corners, looking West.   The Church.   Four Corners, looking South.
Four Corners, looking East.   The School.   Four Corners, looking North.

its lines, including step-ladders, lawn-swings, and a general line of porch goods, such as chairs, stools, settees, etc. A large dairy and hay region contributes greatly to the wealth and happiness of this lovely village. In spite of the more than ordinary discouragements which the agriculturists have suffered this year, the farms of the town of Orwell have been abundantly productive, and the fields of oats and hay on the larger part of the country places in the vicinity of Orwell village have never looked much better than they do this year at harvest time. Society in Orwell is made up of a well-informed, prosperous people. There is no better school in the rural districts anywhere. One commodious church building, which all the people are proud of, was built in 1844 as a union church, and has always been well cared for. It is used by all the worshippers of the village and vicinity, proving that Christianity of all creeds can live together in brotherly love. Orwell village is

afterwards bought the property and carried on tanning until 1884, when the building was allowed to stand idle for about three years, when it was purchased by A. E. Olmstead, who converted it into a chair factory, which two years later he sold to Frank B. Woodbury, the present proprietor. Among the later business and manufacturing interests are the cheese factories of A. E. Olmstead, A. C. McKinney, Alling Stevens, and the Molino cheese factory, W. F. Kenney's grist-mill and Van Auken's cheese-box factory. Orwell is also a great town for the manufacture of spruce ladders, which are sent all over the country, bringing into the town a good many thousands of dollars yearly. Orwell has the following societies and lodges: The Grand Army Post S. M. Olmstead, Ladies' Relief Corps, Odd Fellows' Lodge, with a large membership; Maccabees, Rebecka Lodge, Grangers' Lodge, and also a number of different church societies.

Messenger, Photo.   W. H. LATTIMER & SONS, Orwell, N. Y. (See sketch page 72

The Town of Orwell was formed from Richland, Feb. 28, 1817, and it then included the present town of Boylston, which was set off as a separate town Feb. 7, 1828. A narrow strip was annexed to Orwell, taken from the town of Richland, March 27, 1844. The first settlers were Frederick Eastman and Jesse Merrill, who in 1806 located on the north bank of the Salmon River, one mile below Pekin. Captain George W. Noyes, the first settler in Orwell village, came there in 1807, but soon after moved away. About 1809 Timothy Balch moved from Sandy Creek to Orwell corners, as it was then known, and erected a log house, in which he opened a tavern. Among the later settlers who came to what is now Orwell village, were Orrin Stowell, Ebenezer Robbins, on the hill east of the village, and John Reynolds, on the road to Pekin. Eli Strong, another early settler, was postmaster at Orwell for twenty-four years. In 1818, Nathaniel Beadle and his son John, with five others, settled near the "Corners." In 1808 Silas Maxham settled half a mile east of Pekin and Elias Mason took up his residence near Salmon River Falls. About 1811 Millain Aiken built the first saw-mill in Orwell, it being located on the river near the falls. Soon after, James Hughes placed a trip hammer in operation on a small brook a few rods below Pekin, where he made scythes, axes and other tools. Among others who settled in the town prior to 1812 were Joshua Hollis, near the Sandy Creek line, Silas West, in the Bennett neighborhood, and Eli Strong, Jr., between Orwell village and Pekin. Among those who were living in the town in 1817 were James Wood, John

B. Tully, Allen Gilbert and sons, Edwin and Allen, Jr., on the road to Sandy Creek; Frederick Brooks and Timothy, Jr., and John, sons of Timothy Balch, Sr., in the vicinity of Orwell village; Asa Hewitt, near the river, and the two Lewis families and Perley Wyman, above Pekin. Other settlers prior to 1840 were Nathan F. Montague in 1826, John E. Potter in 1828, and Joseph M. Bonner. Hon. John Parker, who settled in the town in June, 1834, died Aug. 11, 1891. Orimell B. Olmstead settled in the town in the year 1838. The first school in town was taught by Jesse Aiken in 1810. During the summer of 1818 a small frame school house was erected at Orwell village, where school was kept the following winter by Samuel Stowell. The school at Pekin was then being taught by Mr. Wheelock. During that year two school districts were erected in the town. During the War of the Rebellion the town of Orwell sent 184 men to the Union army and navy, all of whom gave a good account of themselves. This number was far in excess of the town's quota. It was also the largest number of men in proportion to the number of inhabitants of any town in the state. It included the following commissioned officers: Captain Burch, John J. Hollis, Captain Orimell B. Olmstead, Alfred N. Beadle, Dr. John S. Stillman and B. F. Lewis. In 1895 there was a very pretty soldiers' monument erected in Orwell, Evergreen Cemetery, at a cost of over $1,600, which was raised by voluntary subscription, in memory of those who went to defend our country.

Messenger, Photo.   [See sketch page 72.
MRS. ORRIN BEADLE'S RESIDENCE, Orwell, N. Y.

Messenger, Photo.   F. B. WOODBURY'S CHAIR FACTORY, Orwell, N. Y.

The F. B. Woodbury Chair Factory at Orwell was started by A. E. Olmstead twenty years ago. Twelve years ago Mr. Woodbury bought the property and began making rockers. Subsequently he added a line of fancy upholstered rockers, which he is now manufacturing in several desirable lines and marketing with the best chair trade. His location at Orwell, convenient for the employment of forty men, which he keeps busy through the year, has its advantages in that his expenses are comparatively light and he is able to make figures in strong competition with the trade. The plant, which is a large one, includes two buildings—one 120 x 40, and the other 40 x 80— each having four floors. It is equipped with 40-horse steam power, and has a present capacity for 100 chairs a day.

The Soldiers' Monument at Orwell village, erected to the memory of 184 citizens of Orwell who fought in the War of the Rebellion in defense of the Union, is one of the handsomest structures of its kind in Central New York. It is made of dark Barre granite, having the total height of 19 feet and one inch and weighs 25 tons. The figure of a soldier resting upon his musket, which is 6 feet and 3 inches high, stands upon a pedestal supported by a cap resting upon a die. A succession of three bases capped by a sub-die, constitutes the foundation. The monument stands upon an elevation 50 feet high, in Evergreen Cemetery, overlooking the main road into the village from the west. Its cost was over $1,500, all of which was raised by the citizens of the village. The monument was dedicated with impressive ceremonies on the Fourth of July, 1894, participated in by over a thousand people, and was at that time presented to S. M. Olmstead Post, No. 387, G. A. R., of Orwell, under whose auspices the project was started and carried out. The unveiling of the monument in the presence of so large concourse of people was the occasion of a tremendous burst of enthusiasm. The inscription on the dies include the names and services of those to whose memory it was raised, the names of new members of the Post and of the committee appointed by the Post to carry out the details of the project; and the following brief explanation:

Veterans.
Erected in Memory of the
184 Soldiers
Of Orwell who Defended
Our Flag on Land and Water
from
1861 . . . . 1865.
Fraternity.   Charity.   Loyalty.

The names of the committee are A. E. Olmstead, A. J. Potter, M. Myers, E. Near and D. Hilton.

On October 14, 1885, the village of Sand Bank (Altmar) was destroyed by fire.

Messenger, Photo.
F. B. WOODBURY AND STAFF OF EMPLOYES, Orwell, N. Y.

Top Row (in the door standing, left to right)—John M. Stowell, Bert Webb, Samuel Bass, C. A. Larned, bookkeeper; Floyd Pratt, Charles Baleh, foreman of finishing department; Charles Barker. Standing (left hand side of the door)—F. B. Woodbury, proprietor; Jasper Finster, R. L. Stevens, superintendent. Inside of window—Pearl Thomas. Standing (right hand side of door)—Foster S. Pratt, W. F. Stowell. Seated on step and window ledge (left to right)—James Miner, Charles Kirch, foreman of cabinet department; Albert Kirch, Wm. Steele, Bert Lobdell, Reuben Carpenter. Seated on the ground (left to right)—Adelbert Babcock, A. B. Woolever, Wm. Joslyn, Arthur Baleh, Ralph W. Pratt, Everett Clemens, E. P. Miner, Day Finster, W. D. Damon, S. W. Aldrich, L. H. Finster, L. A. Potter, W. R. Sparks.

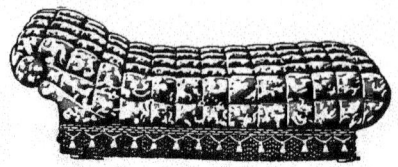

Printed by BoD"in Norderstedt, Germany

9 789353 977214